INTRODUCTION TO
ELECTRONICS

Pam Beasant

Editor: Lisa Watts
Consultant editor: John Hawkins
Consultant: Ian Findlay

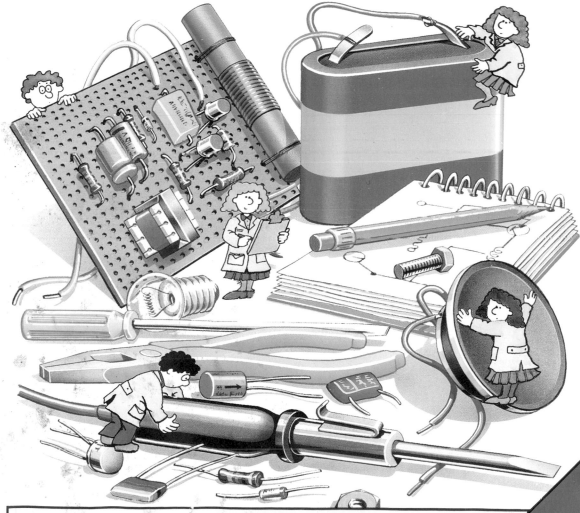

Designed by Siglinde Ruschig, Sue Mims and
Iain Ashman
Illustrated by Martin Newton and Jane Andrews
Additional illustrations by Gerry Browne, Chris Lyon,
Simon Roulstone and Jeremy Banks

Computer program by Chris Oxlade

WITH
COMPUTER
PROGRAM LISTING

Contents

First published in 1985 by Usborne
Publishing Ltd, 20 Garrick Street, London
WC2E 9BJ

Printed in Belgium

About this book

This book is an introduction to the basic principles of electronics. With lots of simple experiments, it shows how electricity is controlled using devices called components. Each experiment is designed to illustrate an important principle of electronics and demonstrate how different components work.

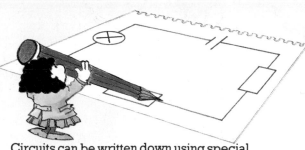

Circuits can be written down using special symbols for each component. You can find out what these symbols are, and how to use them, on page 16.

Components are connected together to make arrangements called electronic circuits. On the following pages, you can build your own circuits, and find out how the circuits inside a complicated piece of equipment make it work.

Later in the book, you can read about the story of electronics – how it began, and what the latest developments are. The invention of the silicon chip, for instance, revolutionized electronics and made it possible to have circuits containing thousands of components on one tiny chip of silicon. Find out more about the chip on pages 32-33.

On page 37, there is a computer program which you can use to help you identify some of the electronic components.

The experiments

At the back of the book, there is a shopping list of the things you need for all the experiments, and advice on where to buy them.

The circuits can be built on a single circuit board, called the experiment board. You can find out how to set up the experiment board on pages 42-43.

To make the circuits, you fix components to the experiment board with a special metal called solder. There are step by step instructions for how to use solder on pages 40-41.

What is electronics?

Electronics is the study of how small electric currents are controlled to make all kinds of electronic equipment work. Although electronics is a young science, it would be hard to imagine a world without televisions, radios, or even computers. Because of electronics, we can travel and communicate quickly and easily all round the world, and astronauts are exploring further and further into space.

Satellites, like the one above, gather and transmit electronic signals from Earth. You can watch live programmes on TV, transmitted by satellite from the other side of the world.

Radios and TVs were invented early this century as the study of electronics progressed. They contain components called transistors which you can use in experiments later in the book.

Computers store and organize millions of electronic instructions and data. You can find out more about the circuits inside a computer on pages 26-27.

Robots do things like building cars and packing sweets in a factory. A robot arm, like the one above, is controlled by a computer.

Components

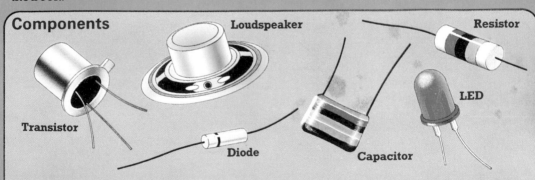

Transistor · Loudspeaker · Diode · Capacitor · Resistor · LED

The building blocks of electronics are called components. There are many different types, used to control electricity in various ways. Some of those used in this book are shown above. As you go through the book, you can find out what each of these components does and how they work together in circuits.

4

About electric current

An electric current is a drift of microscopic particles called electrons along a piece of wire. All substances contain electrons. They are part of the atoms of which everything is made. You, this book and electronic components, are all made of atoms.

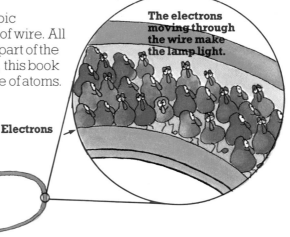

The electrons moving through the wire make the lamp light.

Electrons

Power supply

In certain substances, e.g. metal wire, electrons can be made to move easily by applying a power supply. Substances in which electrons move easily are called conductors.

Making the current flow

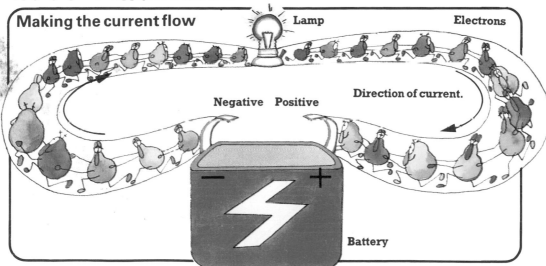

Lamp   Electrons

Negative   Positive

Direction of current.

Battery

A battery is a power supply. It has two terminals. One terminal has a positive charge and the other has a negative charge. Electrons also have a negative charge. When wire is connected to each of the terminals, the electrons in the wire are repelled by the negative terminal and attracted to the positive. This causes the electrons to move through the wire and form an electric current. The force from the battery which makes the electrons move is called electro-motive force (e.m.f. for short), or voltage. It is measured in volts.

The first battery

In 1800, Alessandro Volta made the first battery out of two different kinds of metal and some acid. He was the first person to show that we could make electricity flow and control it ourselves. Voltage is named after him.

5

Building circuits

A circuit is a pathway along which electric current can flow. Every circuit needs two things: a power supply and something to conduct the electric current. On these two pages, there are some simple circuits to build to find out more about electric current.

Bulb and battery circuit

Take a battery, a screw-in lamp and holder and two pieces of wire. Strip 1cm (½″) of plastic off the ends of the wires. *

Twist one end of each wire round a battery terminal, then touch the lamp's terminals with both wires. It should light up because you have made a circuit.

Now take one of the wires off the battery and the lamp will go out. This is because you have broken the circuit path for the electric current.

How the circuit works

Batteries come in all shapes and sizes and their voltage is usually written on them.

You must always have a component in a circuit to use the current, or the battery might be damaged.

Imagine the battery as a highly charged robot. When the robot is not touching a conductor, no current can flow and the lamp does not light. For current to flow, there must be a complete circuit from the positive to the negative terminal of the battery.

As soon as the robot touches both ends of the wire, the current flows and the lamp lights. A battery is full of force all the time, but only uses it when you make a circuit by connecting a conductor to the two terminals.

See page 43 for how to do this.

Conducting the current

Here is another experiment to try. Take an extra piece of wire and any objects around you. Connect each object to the lamp and battery as shown in the picture, and note whether the lamp lights.

If the lamp lights, you are using a conductor of electricity. Current can flow through a conductor, so the circuit is complete. If the lamp does not light, you are using an insulator which does not allow current to flow.

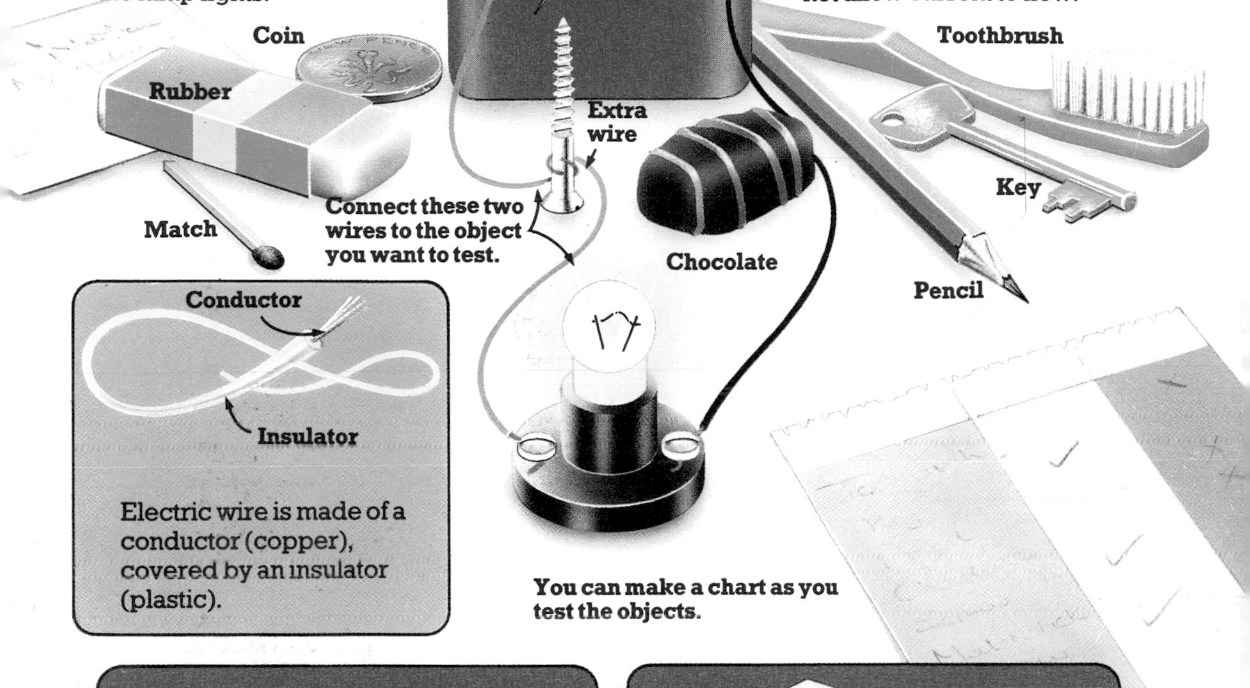

Sticky tape

Coin

Rubber

Toothbrush

Extra wire

Key

Match

Connect these two wires to the object you want to test.

Chocolate

Pencil

Conductor

Insulator

Electric wire is made of a conductor (copper), covered by an insulator (plastic).

You can make a chart as you test the objects.

Printed circuit boards

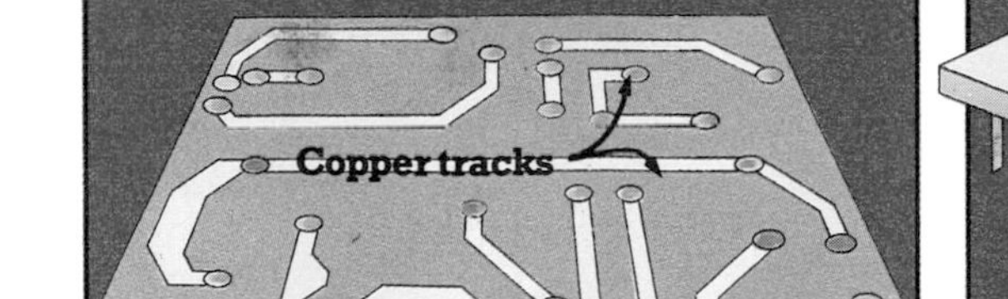

Copper tracks

Fibre glass

In most electronic equipment, the components for the circuits are arranged on a printed circuit board. This is made of a substance, normally fibre glass, which will not conduct electric current. The board has copper tracks on it to carry the current between the components.

The chip

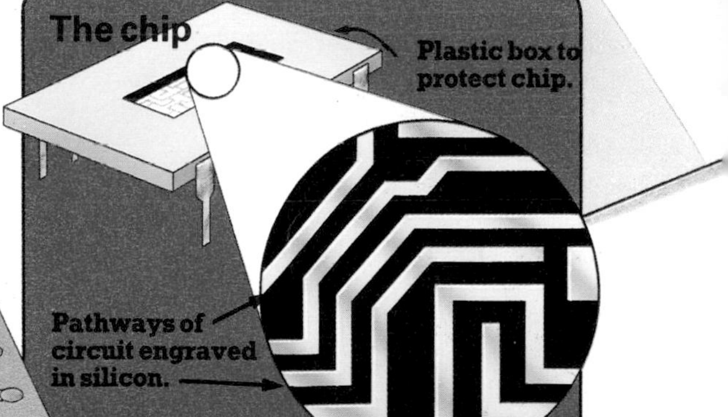

Plastic box to protect chip.

Pathways of circuit engraved in silicon.

A chip is a tiny slice of silicon engraved with hundreds, or sometimes thousands, of microscopic components. They are connected together by pathways which conduct the current through the silicon. The proper name for a silicon chip is an integrated circuit, or IC.

7

Controlling the current

Electronics is all about controlling electric current to make it do something useful. You do this by building circuits using electronic components.

The voltage in the battery generates a current and each component controls the current in a different way. The special way in which components are connected in a circuit makes a piece of equipment work.

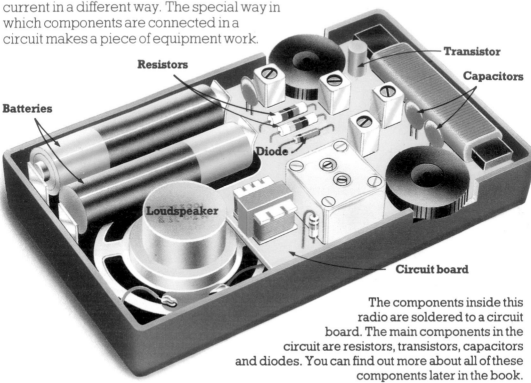

The components inside this radio are soldered to a circuit board. The main components in the circuit are resistors, transistors, capacitors and diodes. You can find out more about all of these components later in the book.

More about voltage and current

The amount of current generated by the battery depends on the voltage of the battery. Common voltages are 4.5 volts, 6 volts or 9 volts. These are usually written on the battery. A small voltage generates a small current and a larger voltage generates a larger current.

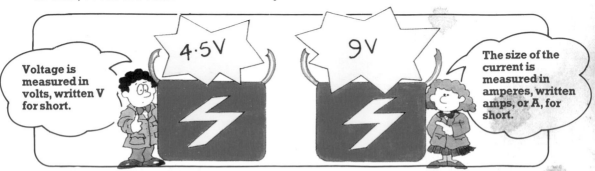

Voltage is measured in volts, written V for short.

The size of the current is measured in amperes, written amps, or A, for short.

Voltage is also referred to as potential difference (or p.d.). For example, a 4.5V battery has a potential difference of 4.5V between its terminals. This difference refers to a difference of electrical pressure. At the positive terminal of the battery the voltage is 4.5V, and at the negative, it is 0V. There is a pressure difference of 4.5V between the terminals. It is this difference that causes a voltage and a voltage cannot exist without it.

Resistance

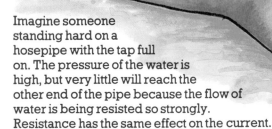

Current and voltage are two of the main ingredients in a circuit. The third is resistance. Resistance is the way certain substances restrict the flow of electrons and so reduce the strength of the current. This is one of the main ways of controlling the current in a circuit.

Imagine someone standing hard on a hosepipe with the tap full on. The pressure of the water is high, but very little will reach the other end of the pipe because the flow of water is being resisted so strongly. Resistance has the same effect on the current.

Resistance is measured in ohms. Scientists use the Greek symbol Ω for short. This stands for the Greek letter *omega*.

Resistor

All components resist the current to some degree, but components called resistors are specially made to cut down the current. They are used to control the current and the voltage for another component, or to prevent a delicate component from being damaged by too much current. Most resistors contain carbon, which does not conduct electricity very well.

Current, voltage and resistance

Current, voltage and resistance are all related and depend on each other. The strength of current flowing in a circuit depends on the battery voltage, and on how much resistance there is in the circuit.

Ammeter measures current.

Voltmeter measures voltage.

Ohmmeter measures resistance.

You can measure current, voltage and resistance using special testmeters. They are used to check circuits and component values, or to find the faulty area of a circuit.

Which way is the current flowing?

Early scientists believed the current flowed from positive to negative, although it is now thought that it flows in the opposite direction. The first idea is kept because so many laws were written round it. It is called "conventional current" to save confusion.

Warning

Mains electricity in your home has a very high voltage. In some countries it is 110 volts, and in others, as high as 240 volts. This is enough to kill you if you come into direct contact with it. Never take apart electrical equipment in your home, and never use mains electricity for any of your projects.

Looking at resistors

Resistors are used to cut down the flow of current in circuits. Resistance is measured in ohms (written Ω). In circuits it can vary from just a few ohms, to millions. You can work out a resistor's value from the coloured stripes painted on it. The colours are part of a special colour code which is shown on the right.

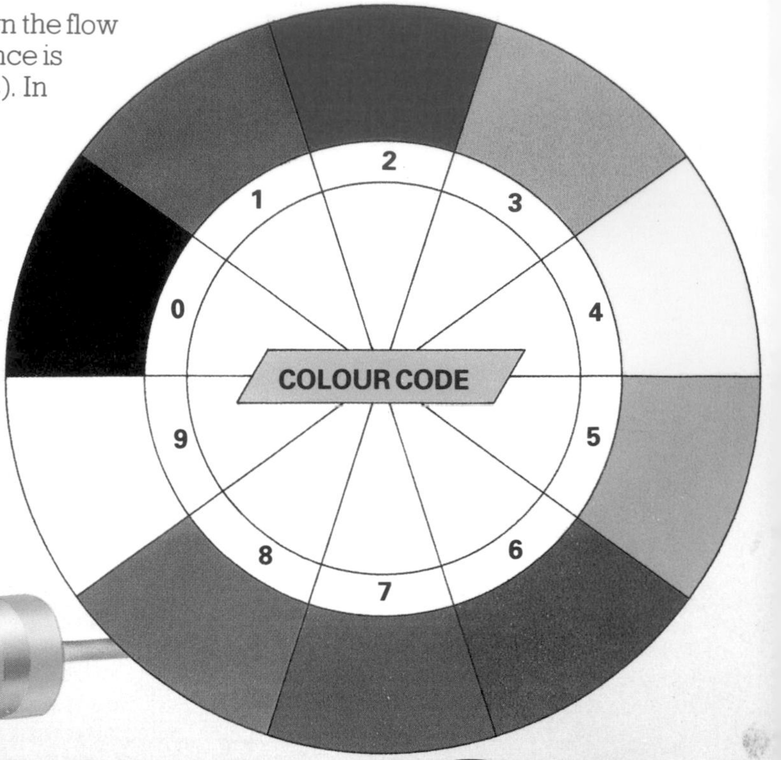

COLOUR CODE

0 1 2 3 4 5 6 7 8 9

Reading the colour code

The three stripes closest together are the colour code stripes. Start at the end furthest from the fourth stripe and match the colours to the chart.

1 2 3   4

Start here

The first two stripes give you the first two numbers of the resistor's value. The third tells you how many 0s to add onto the numbers.* There is a computer program for working out colour codes on page 37.

Green, green, black =55 ohms

Red, red, blue= 22,000,000 ohms.

Try working out the values of these resistors. (Answers on page 45.)

Ohm's law

You can calculate the current, the voltage or the resistance of a circuit using a formula called Ohm's law. To use the formula, you need to know the values of two of the quantities.

| Voltage (Volts) | = | Current (Amps) | x | Resistance (Ohms) |

It is easy to use the formula if you think of it as a triangle. Volts are always on top, and current and resistance on the bottom two corners. (In Ohm's law, I represents current.)

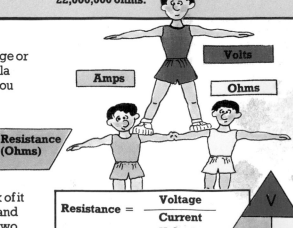

Volts

Amps

Ohms

$$\text{Resistance} = \frac{\text{Voltage}}{\text{Current}}$$

$$\text{Current} = \frac{\text{Voltage}}{\text{Resistance}}$$

V / I / R

*You can find out about the fourth stripe on page 29.

Resistors in circuits

Note the brightness of the bulb.

Brown, black, brown resistor.

Here are some circuits to test resistors. You need a 4.5V battery, a 3.5V/60mA lamp* and holder, three pieces of wire and two 100Ω resistors. First, connect just the lamp and battery.

Then add one resistor to the circuit. The lamp is dimmer in this circuit because the resistor is cutting down the current.

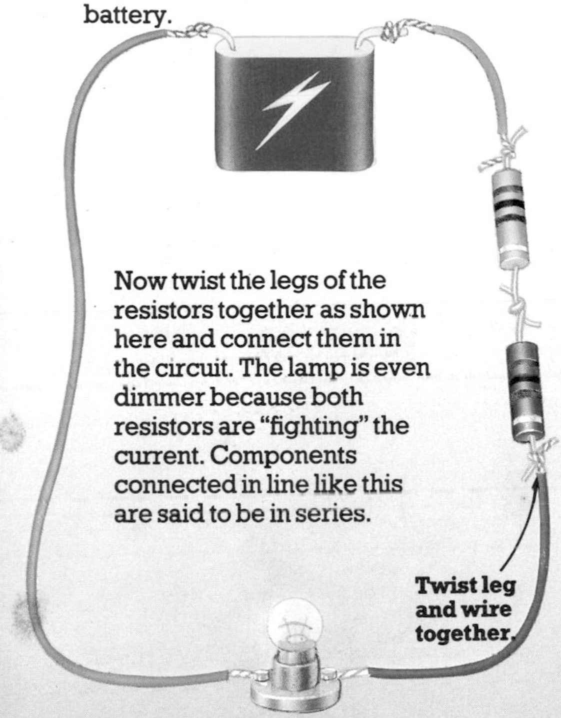

Now twist the legs of the resistors together as shown here and connect them in the circuit. The lamp is even dimmer because both resistors are "fighting" the current. Components connected in line like this are said to be in series.

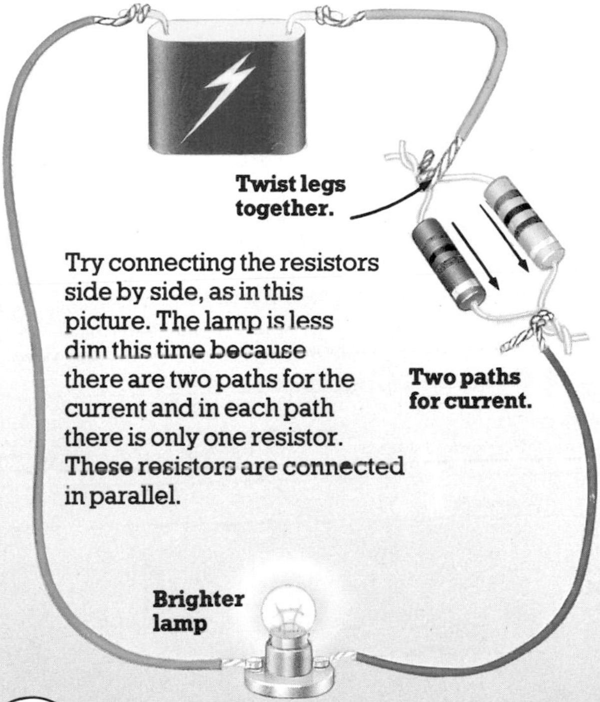

Twist leg and wire together.

Twist legs together.

Try connecting the resistors side by side, as in this picture. The lamp is less dim this time because there are two paths for the current and in each path there is only one resistor. These resistors are connected in parallel.

Two paths for current.

Brighter lamp

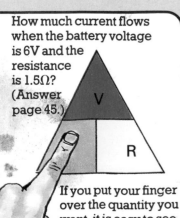

How much current flows when the battery voltage is 6V and the resistance is 1.5Ω? (Answer page 45.)

V

R

If you put your finger over the quantity you want, it is easy to see how the formula works.

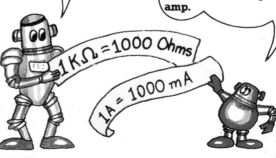

High resistances are measured in kilohms (KΩ) and megohms (MΩ). 1KΩ is a thousand ohms and 1MΩ is a million.

Small currents are measured in milliamps, written mA. There are a thousand milliamps in one amp.

1KΩ = 1000 Ohms

1A = 1000 mA

11

*This lamp is suitable for small currents.

Investigating electronics

The best way to understand electronics is to build some simple circuits to see how components work. On these two pages there is a circuit to build to test a component called an LED, which glows like a tiny lamp. You can find out what you need, and how to set up an experiment board to use for the projects in this book, on page 42.

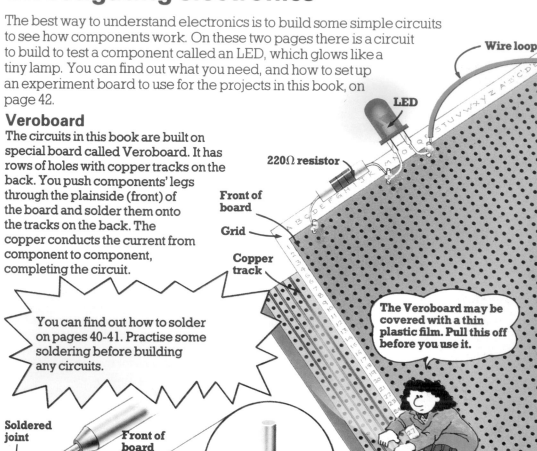

Wire loop

LED

220Ω resistor

Front of board

Grid

Copper track

Back of board

Holes

The Veroboard may be covered with a thin plastic film. Pull this off before you use it.

Veroboard

The circuits in this book are built on special board called Veroboard. It has rows of holes with copper tracks on the back. You push components' legs through the plainside (front) of the board and solder them onto the tracks on the back. The copper conducts the current from component to component, completing the circuit.

You can find out how to solder on pages 40-41. Practise some soldering before building any circuits.

Soldered joint

Front of board

Solder pin

You can solder the components onto solder pins rather than to the board itself. This makes it easier to change the components for different circuits.

You push the pins through from the back to the front of the board, then solder them to the tracks. You solder the components to the pins on the front of the board.

Looking at LEDs

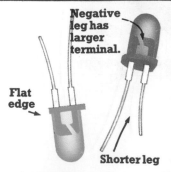

Negative leg has larger terminal.

Flat edge

Shorter leg

LED stands for light emitting diode. A diode is like a one-way street for electricity. Current can only flow through it in one direction. An LED is a special kind of diode that lights up and is used in a circuit to show that a current is flowing.

An LED sometimes has one leg shorter than the other. The shorter leg is called the negative leg (−ve) and the longer one is the positive (+ve). The negative leg might also have a flat edge on the plastic cap to help you identify it. It is important to connect the LED's legs the right way round in a circuit.

Making the LED circuit

Things you need

Experiment board with grid (see page 42)

LED

220Ω resistor (red, red, brown)

2 pieces of wire

Solder pins

Soldering kit (see page 40)

You can find the right holes for the components more quickly by making a grid. Find out how on page 42.

1

Back

C47   H¹47

Push solder pins into holes **C47** and **H¹47**, from the back to the front of the board. Solder the pins to the tracks.

2

– + Front A1.

Now, on the front of the board, twist a stripped piece of wire onto each pin and solder it in place. These wires are for the battery.

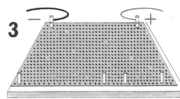

3

– +

↑ **H¹**   **Q1**↑ ↑ **L1** ↑ **C1**

Take four solder pins and push them into holes **C1, L1, Q1** and **H¹1**. Secure them to the tracks with blobs of solder.

4

– +

Negative leg

Q1   **L1**

On the front of the board, solder the negative (shorter) leg of the LED onto the pin in hole **Q1**, and the positive (longer) leg on pin **L1**.

5

– +

H¹1   **Q1**   **L1**   **C1**

Now twist a short piece of wire onto pins **Q1** and **H¹1** and solder the 220Ω resistor onto pins **C1** and **L1**.

6

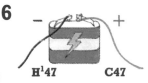

– +

H¹47   **C47**

Connect the wire from **C47** to the positive(+ve) terminal, and the **H¹47** wire to the negative (−ve). The LED should light up.*

When you wire up a battery, the current flows round the circuit from the positive terminal to the negative. Try swapping the wires on the battery terminals so that pin **C47** is connected to the negative terminal. The LED stays off because the current cannot flow through it in that direction.

How the LED works

Imagine a line of elephants walking nose to tail. If one of them is facing the wrong way, it stops the whole line from moving forwards. The LED has the same effect on the current. If you connect the negative leg to the positive path from the battery, the LED has a high resistance and the current cannot flow.

*If it does not work, turn to the faults checklist on pages 46-47.

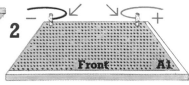

Storing electric charge

Components called capacitors fill up with electricity when connected to a power supply, then store the charge for a while. They are used, for instance, in a television, to build up and store the high voltages needed to make it work. When charged, the voltage across a capacitor is equal to that of the battery or power supply.

This is one of the reasons why it is very dangerous to touch the inside of electrical equipment that uses mains electricity. The capacitors remain highly charged even after the appliance has been unplugged.

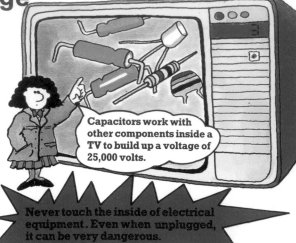

Capacitors work with other components inside a TV to build up a voltage of 25,000 volts.

Never touch the inside of electrical equipment. Even when unplugged, it can be very dangerous.

Types of capacitor

Don't worry if your capacitors do not look like any of these as long as they are the correct values.

Stripe on case shows negative leg.

Capacitors come in all shapes and sizes. Some are called electrolytic and have a positive and negative leg which must be connected the right way in a circuit.

A capacitor's value is measured in farads which are large units. Microfarads are used more often. They are written μF. 1,000,000μF make 1 farad.

Not all capacitors are electrolytic. Usually those with a small value (less than 1μF) can be connected any way round in a circuit.

Make a capacitor circuit

You can test a capacitor's ability to store electric charge on your experiment board. You need a 100 microfarad electrolytic capacitor (written 100μF).

1 Unsolder the wire on pins **Q1** and **H^{1}1**, and twist the capacitor's negative leg onto **H^{1}1** and its positive leg onto **Q1**. Make sure they are the right way round.

2 When you connect up the battery (make sure it's the right way round) the LED should light for a second as the capacitor charges up, then go out when it is fully charged.*

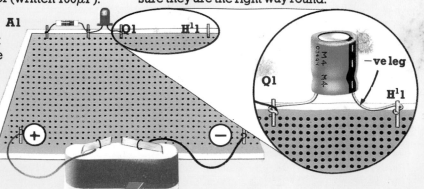

A1

Q1   H^{1}1

−ve leg

Q1

H^{1}1

14

y

*If the circuit does not work, see pages 46-47.

A.c., d.c.

Battery current is called direct current (d.c.) because it flows constantly in one direction. The electricity that flows in the mains is called alternating current, or a.c., because it flows backwards and forwards many times a second.

Once charged, a capacitor blocks d.c. but not a.c. This is why, in the first stage of the experiment below, the LED goes out.

With a.c., the capacitor constantly charges and discharges as the current goes backwards and forwards.

Tuning radios

Variable capacitors are used in radios to tune into stations. They are also used for filtering out unwanted electric signals.

3

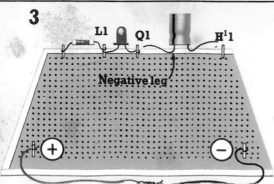

L1 Q1 H¹1

Negative leg

Twist wires together.

Disconnect the battery wires and twist them together so that the circuit is still complete. Take out the capacitor, turn it round and replace it on the pins. (Do not let its legs touch each other.)

4

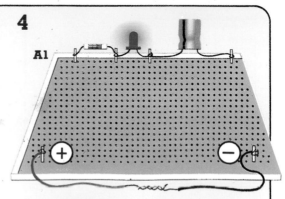

A1

The LED should light for an instant as it uses the charge stored in the capacitor. It had to be turned round to allow the current to flow in the right direction through the one-way LED.

Symbols and diagrams

When circuit designers are planning a circuit, they draw a diagram of it on paper first. The diagram is like a map from which the circuit can be built. They use symbols to represent the different components.

The symbols are closely related to what the components look like, or how they work. The chart on the right shows all the components you have used already, with their circuit symbols.

Circuit diagrams

The circuits you have already made on the experiment board are drawn below. Use the chart on the right to find out what the symbols mean.

LED circuit

Capacitor circuit

From now on, the circuit diagrams are given alongside the circuits, or at the back of the book.

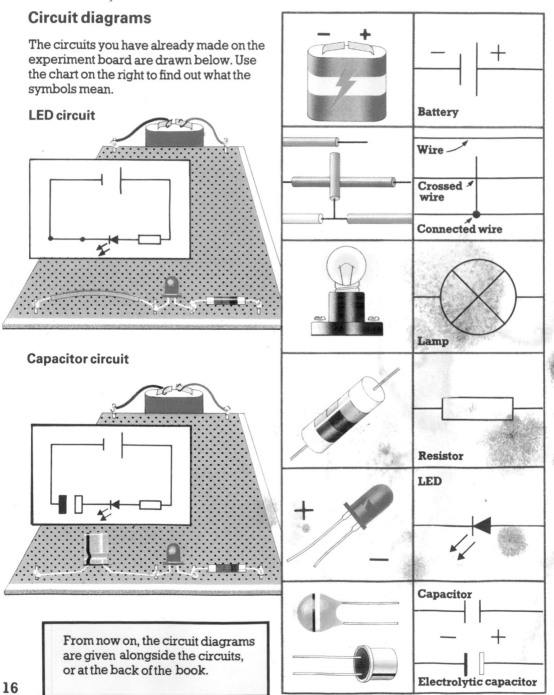

	Battery
	Wire
	Crossed wire
	Connected wire
	Lamp
	Resistor
	LED
	Capacitor
	Electrolytic capacitor

Introducing transistors

Transistor radios are named after components called transistors. The invention of transistors, in 1952, made it possible to build battery-powered, portable radios instead of large wirelesses made with components called valves.

In a circuit, a transistor can switch the current on and off. It also amplifies the current, which means it makes the current bigger.

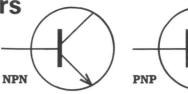

NPN   **PNP**

There are two types of transistor – NPN and PNP. The circuit symbols are shown above. "N" and "P" refer to the substance inside a transistor. The NPN transistor is the most common and it is the type used in this book.

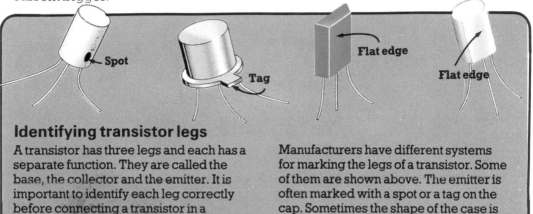

Spot   Tag   Flat edge   Flat edge

Identifying transistor legs

A transistor has three legs and each has a separate function. They are called the base, the collector and the emitter. It is important to identify each leg correctly before connecting a transistor in a circuit.

Manufacturers have different systems for marking the legs of a transistor. Some of them are shown above. The emitter is often marked with a spot or a tag on the cap. Sometimes the shape of the case is important.

How a transistor works

A transistor can be made to switch on and off by applying a small current to the base leg of the transistor. These pictures show how, when there is no current to the base, no current can flow between the collector and the emitter and the transistor is off.

A small current to the base enables the transistor to conduct current from the collector to the emitter, and allows a larger current to flow through the transistor. Components connected to the collector can use this larger current.

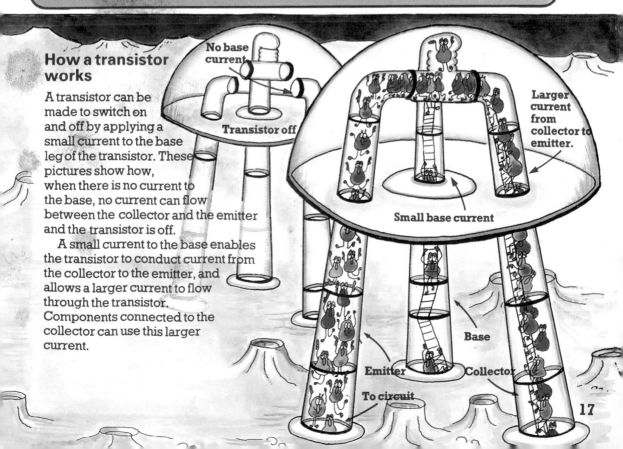

No base current

Transistor off

Larger current from collector to emitter.

Small base current

Base

Emitter   Collector

To circuit

17

Transistors in circuits

A transistor, like most other components, is not much use on its own, although it forms a vital part of most circuits. On this page you can build a circuit using a transistor as a switch for the LED. The chart opposite shows how the circuit works.

1

Negative path

Positive path

H¹11 R11 C11 H¹1 S1 R6

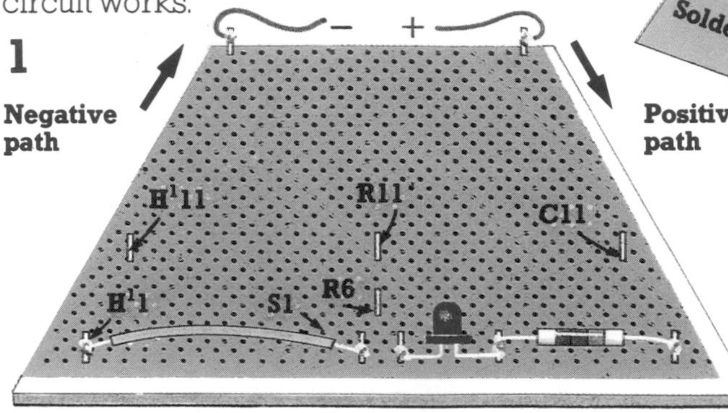

To connect the LED and resistor to the negative path of the circuit, solder a pin into **S1**, and a piece of wire onto pins **S1** and **H¹1**.

Now push four solder pins, from the back to the front of the board, in holes **R6, R11, C11** and **H¹11**. Secure each pin to the track with solder.

2

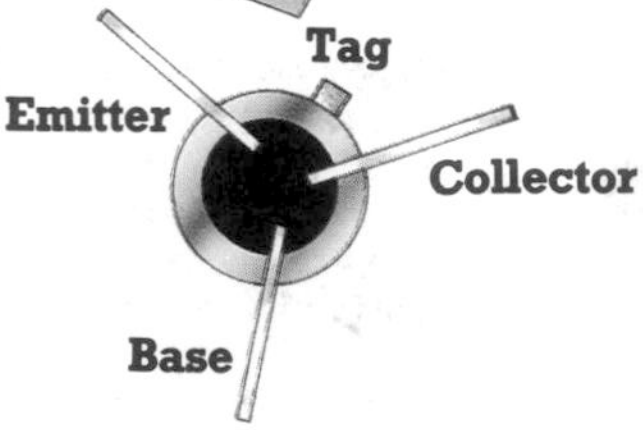

Tag Emitter Collector Base

Carefully identify the legs on the transistor. If you connect the transistor wrongly it could be damaged and the circuit will not work.

3

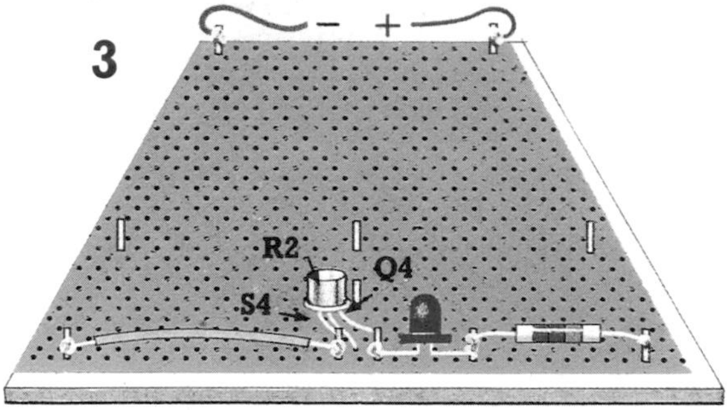

R2 Q4 S4

Place the emitter in hole **S4**, the collector in hole **Q4** and the base in **R2**. Turn the board over and solder the legs to the tracks. The transistor does not need to go on pins because it will not be moved.

4

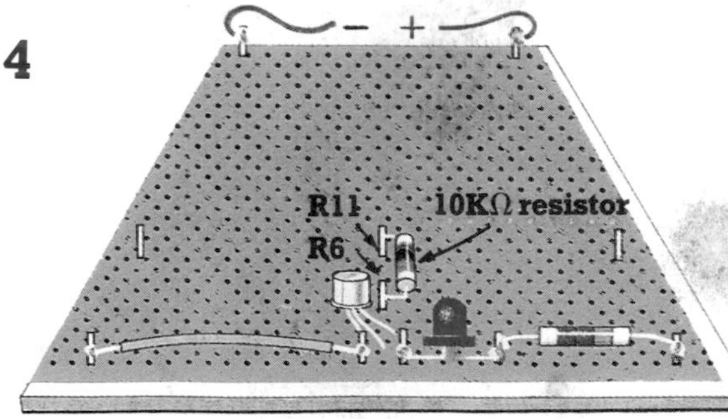

R11 10KΩ resistor R6

You need a 10KΩ resistor (brown, black, orange), at the base of the transistor, to cut down the current. Solder it onto the pins at holes **R6** and **R11**.

5

Solder one end of a stripped piece of wire onto the pin at **R11** to make a wander lead. Connect up the battery (make sure it is the right way round). Then try touching the pins at **C11** and **H¹11** with the wander lead.

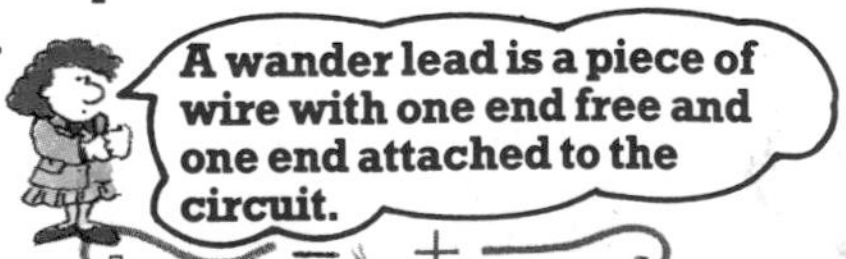

> A wander lead is a piece of wire with one end free and one end attached to the circuit.

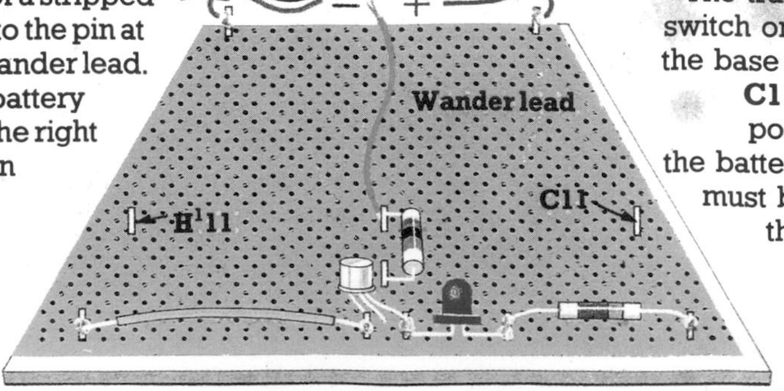

The transistor will only switch on the LED when the base leg connects to **C11. C11** is on the positive path from the battery and the base must be connected to the positive path.

Wander lead H¹11 C11

18

More about the transistor circuit

The chart below shows how the current flows round the transistor circuit on the opposite page. Follow its route from the positive terminal of the battery round to the negative.

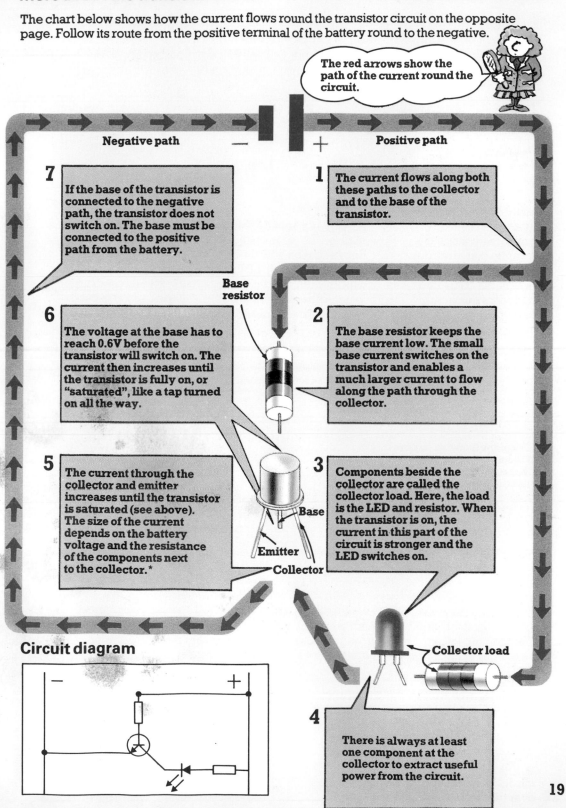

The red arrows show the path of the current round the circuit.

Negative path — + **Positive path**

7 If the base of the transistor is connected to the negative path, the transistor does not switch on. The base must be connected to the positive path from the battery.

1 The current flows along both these paths to the collector and to the base of the transistor.

Base resistor

6 The voltage at the base has to reach 0.6V before the transistor will switch on. The current then increases until the transistor is fully on, or "saturated", like a tap turned on all the way.

2 The base resistor keeps the base current low. The small base current switches on the transistor and enables a much larger current to flow along the path through the collector.

5 The current through the collector and emitter increases until the transistor is saturated (see above). The size of the current depends on the battery voltage and the resistance of the components next to the collector.*

3 Components beside the collector are called the collector load. Here, the load is the LED and resistor. When the transistor is on, the current in this part of the circuit is stronger and the LED switches on.

Base

Emitter

Collector

Circuit diagram

Collector load

4 There is always at least one component at the collector to extract useful power from the circuit.

*See Ohm's law, pages 10-11.

19

Special resistors

The circuits on these pages use some special resistors to control the transistor. There are three kinds and each works like an ordinary resistor, but its resistance can be varied by light or heat, or by hand. Below, you can find out about each of them and their uses. There are also some circuits to build on the experiment board.

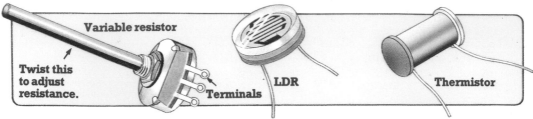

Variable resistor
Twist this to adjust resistance.
Terminals
LDR
Thermistor

Variable resistor
A variable resistor is used to control the voltage in a circuit so that a transistor, for example, is just on or just off. Volume controls on TVs and radios are variable resistors. Some are also called potentiometers.

LDR
An LDR is a light dependent resistor. Its value changes depending on how much light is falling on it. LDRs are used in camera light meters, to detect the amount of light when you are taking a picture.

Thermistor
A thermistor's resistance depends on how hot it is. Usually it has a high resistance when hot. It is sometimes used in fire alarms and in central heating thermostats.

Testing the variable resistor
You can use a variable resistor on your experiment board to control the voltage at the base of the transistor.

Things you need
Experiment board
Variable resistor (1 megohm)
10KΩ resistor
Soldering kit
2 short wires

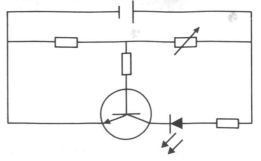

1 Unsolder the wire on pins C11 and R11. Solder the 10KΩ resistor onto pins R11 and H¹11.

Variable resistor

10KΩ resistor R11 C11

H¹11

A1

2 Solder a short wire to the middle terminal of the variable resistor and another wire to either of the other terminals. Solder the wires to pins C11 and R11.

As you adjust the variable resistor you are changing the voltage between the base and the emitter of the transistor. When the voltage reaches 0.6V, the transistor switches on and the LED lights up. As the voltage increases, the LED gets brighter as the transistor becomes saturated.

Circuit diagram
Here is the diagram for the circuit above. In this circuit, the variable resistor and the resistor on pins **R11** and **H¹11** are called a voltage divider. They are sharing the voltage so that a small current can be tapped off to the base of the transistor. You can find out more about voltage dividers over the page.

Transistor gain

While the transistor is becoming saturated, the collector current is always a fixed number of times bigger than the base current because of the way the transistor amplifies.

The currents increase together until the transistor is saturated (see page 19). This is called transistor gain and you can work it out using the transistor gain formula shown opposite.

Circuit designers use this formula when they are working out how much current a circuit needs, and what values of resistors to use.

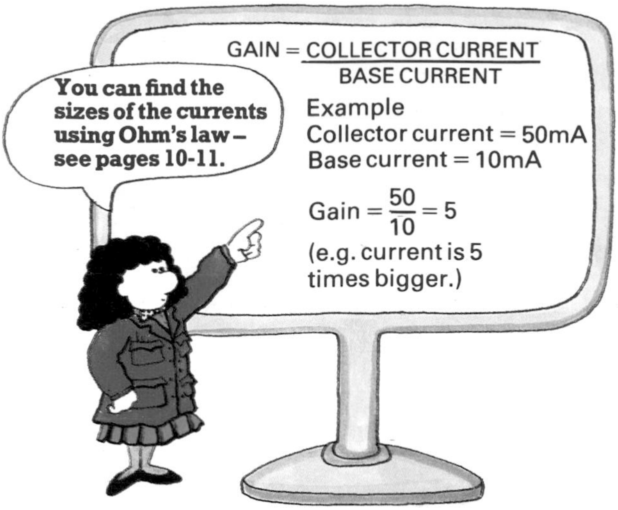

You can find the sizes of the currents using Ohm's law – see pages 10-11.

$$\text{GAIN} = \frac{\text{COLLECTOR CURRENT}}{\text{BASE CURRENT}}$$

Example
Collector current = 50mA
Base current = 10mA

$$\text{Gain} = \frac{50}{10} = 5$$

(e.g. current is 5 times bigger.)

Testing the LDR

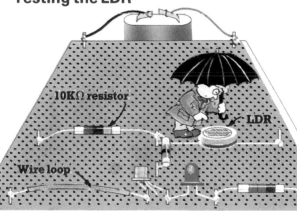

10KΩ resistor

LDR

Wire loop

A1

To test the LDR, unsolder the variable resistor and put the LDR in its place. In the dark its resistance is high, so the LED and the transistor will be off. Cup your hand right over the LDR and watch the LED dim and then go out. This is because you have increased the LDR's resistance by plunging it into darkness. The LDR is dividing the voltage with the 10KΩ resistor.*

The thermistor

Sprinkler

A thermistor can be used in a fire alarm to set the bell ringing and switch on a sprinkler when it reaches a certain temperature.

Try replacing the LDR with a thermistor. To warm it, carefully hold the hot bit of the soldering iron near it. The LED will gradually go off because the thermistor's resistance increases as you heat it.

Buzzers
In all three of the above circuits you could change the collector load (the LED and the resistor on **C1** and **L1**) for a buzzing device called a piezo-electric sounder. It will start and stop sounding as you vary the resistance of the circuit and the transistor switches on and off.

*See next page for more about voltage dividers.

More about voltage: voltage dividers

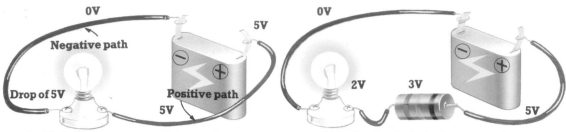

In all circuits, current, voltage and resistance are closely related. On the positive path from the battery, the voltage equals the battery's, but after passing through a component, it drops to 0V on the negative path.

Across one component, the voltage also equals the battery's, but when several components are connected in series,* the drop to 0V then takes place over all the components. The voltage across each depends on its resistance. The components are sharing the battery voltage, and together they are called a voltage divider.

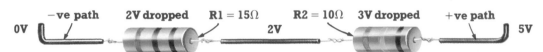

You can calculate how much voltage is dropped by each component using Ohm's law. In the example above, the total resistance of R1 and R2 is 25 ohms, and the battery voltage is 5 volts. To work out how much current is flowing, the formula is $I = V/R$, so the current must be 0.2 amps (5/25).

From this you can calculate the voltage dropped across each resistor ($V = I \times R$). Three volts are dropped across R1 (0.2 × 15) and two volts across R2 (0.2 × 10). So there are two volts across the path between the two resistors. You can use this lower voltage to tap off a small current for other components, such as a transistor which only needs a small base current.

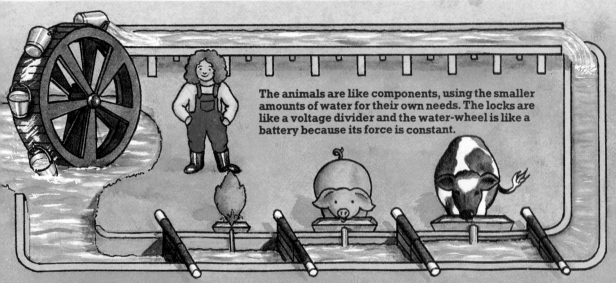

The animals are like components, using the smaller amounts of water for their own needs. The locks are like a voltage divider and the water-wheel is like a battery because its force is constant.

This picture shows the principle of voltage division in another way. A farmer has designed lock gates so that she can tap off the right amount of water to fill the troughs of the cow, the pig and the hen. Whereas the cow needs a lot of water, the hen only needs a little. The water's force is slightly less at each lock gate, but then it flows back to the water-wheel which sends it back round the circuit with the same force as before.

*See pages 10-11.

Switching on large currents

The amplified current and voltage from a transistor can turn on buzzers and LEDs, but it is sometimes not strong enough for other components. A relay is an electrically-controlled switch that can supply a new, larger current to components which need more power. They are also used to direct current along different routes, rather like switching points on a train set.

A relay contains an electro-magnet, that is, metal that can be magnetized and de-magnetized by electricity. It has an iron core with a coil of wire wound round it many times. A small current from a transistor is enough to magnetize it.

Inside the relay, there are sets of contacts that switch the current on and off and are either open or closed. When the contacts are open, no current can flow and when they are closed, it can.

Each contact can be wired to a different area of the same circuit, or even to completely different circuits. When the relay is off, this is its "normal" condition and the contacts are either "normally open" (n/o) or "normally closed" (n/c) – it varies with different relays.

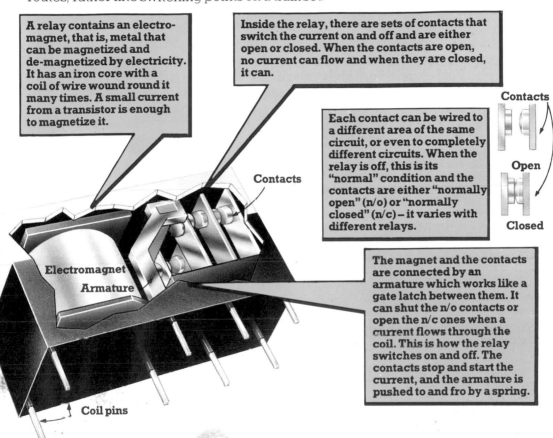

Contacts

Open

Closed

Contacts

Electromagnet

Armature

The magnet and the contacts are connected by an armature which works like a gate latch between them. It can shut the n/o contacts or open the n/c ones when a current flows through the coil. This is how the relay switches on and off. The contacts stop and start the current, and the armature is pushed to and fro by a spring.

Coil pins

If you wire up a battery to the magnet pins (those at one end by themselves), you can hear the relay clicking as it switches. (There is a list of the types of relays you can use on pages 38-39.)

The relay coil produces a high voltage when it switches off. This voltage is strong enough to damage other components in the circuit, such as transistors. A diode is used to control this current to prevent any damage. Some relays are made with a diode already inside them.

Using relays

In the past, thousands of relays were used to switch telephone calls from the exchange to their destination. They were also used to switch traffic lights. Now, modern systems use transistor-based switches on chips which are more reliable and efficient. The telephone exchange, for instance, can handle more telephone calls, more quickly. You are less likely to be cut off or to get a crossed line.

Two-transistor circuits

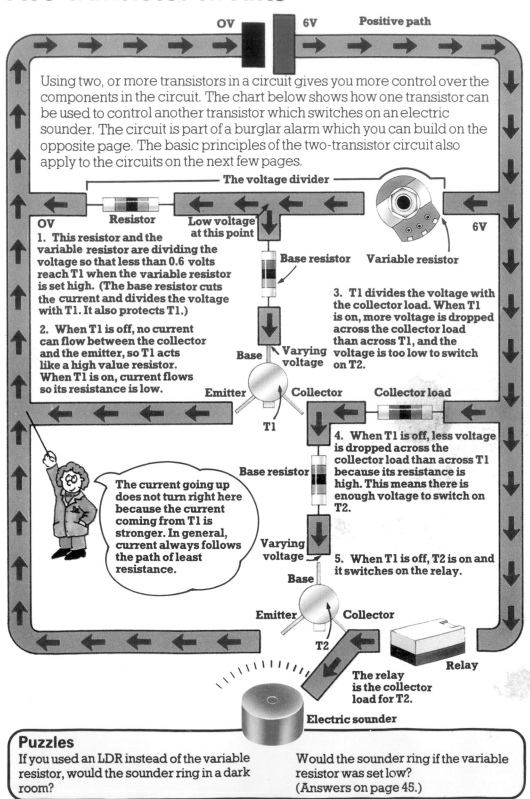

OV   6V   **Positive path**

Using two, or more transistors in a circuit gives you more control over the components in the circuit. The chart below shows how one transistor can be used to control another transistor which switches on an electric sounder. The circuit is part of a burglar alarm which you can build on the opposite page. The basic principles of the two-transistor circuit also apply to the circuits on the next few pages.

The voltage divider

OV   **Resistor**   **Low voltage at this point**   **Variable resistor**   6V

Base resistor

1. This resistor and the variable resistor are dividing the voltage so that less than 0.6 volts reach T1 when the variable resistor is set high. (The base resistor cuts the current and divides the voltage with T1. It also protects T1.)

2. When T1 is off, no current can flow between the collector and the emitter, so T1 acts like a high value resistor. When T1 is on, current flows so its resistance is low.

3. T1 divides the voltage with the collector load. When T1 is on, more voltage is dropped across the collector load than across T1, and the voltage is too low to switch on T2.

Base   **Varying voltage**

Emitter   **Collector**   **Collector load**

T1

The current going up does not turn right here because the current coming from T1 is stronger. In general, current always follows the path of least resistance.

Base resistor

4. When T1 is off, less voltage is dropped across the collector load than across T1 because its resistance is high. This means there is enough voltage to switch on T2.

Varying voltage

5. When T1 is off, T2 is on and it switches on the relay.

Base

Emitter   **Collector**

T2

The relay is the collector load for T2.

Relay

Electric sounder

Puzzles

If you used an LDR instead of the variable resistor, would the sounder ring in a dark room?

Would the sounder ring if the variable resistor was set low? (Answers on page 45.)

Make a burglar alarm

This burglar alarm circuit is controlled by two transistors, as described on the opposite page. To build it, solder the components at the places listed at the bottom of the page. It is quite complicated, so follow the instructions carefully.*

To use the alarm, you need to build a pressure mat. This is like a switch which is wired to the circuit. If a burglar steps on it, the circuit is complete and the sounder rings.

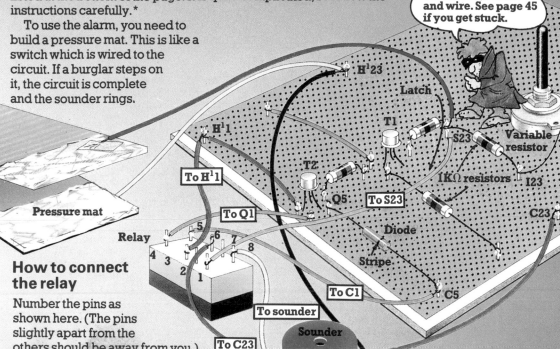

Try designing a pressure mat using cardboard, tin foil and wire. See page 45 if you get stuck.

Pressure mat

H¹23
Latch
T1
S23
Variable resistor
To H¹1
H¹1
T2
1KΩ resistors
I23
Q5
To S23
C23
To Q1
Relay
5 6 7 8
4 3 2 1
Diode
Stripe
To C1
C5
To sounder
Sounder
To C23
+ve terminal

How to connect the relay

Number the pins as shown here. (The pins slightly apart from the others should be away from you.) Solder wires carefully on to all the pins except 2 and 7 as shown.

The relay pins are fragile – take care when soldering.

Place the pressure mat by a window or a door. Set the variable resistor so that its resistance is low and T1 is on. When someone steps on the mat, T1 goes off, T2 switches on and the sounder goes on. It stays on because one of the relay's normally open contacts is being used to keep the sounder ringing. This is called "latching" the circuit. The latch wire is connected between pin 1 of the relay and the base of T1, which keeps the voltage of T1 low and the sounder on.**

Things you need		Board positions	
6V or 9V battery		C47(+ve)	H¹47(−ve)
1MΩ variable resistor		C24	I23
10KΩ resistor		S23	S18
1KΩ resistor		I23	S23
Transistor T1 – Base		S14	
(BC 108)	Collector	R16	
	Emitter	T16	
1KΩ resistor		C13	R13
Pressure mat wires		S23	H¹23
Wire loop		T13	H¹11
Diode (IN4001-6) Stripe towards C5		Q5	C5
Piezo-electric sounder –			
	−ve terminal	H¹23	
	+ve terminal	Relay pin 8	
Relay		See pages 38-39	

Diodes

This circuit uses a new component called a diode. Current can only flow one way through a diode. There is always a stripe to show which way round to connect it. The current flows through the diode towards the stripe. The diode protects T2 from the high voltages fed back by the relay.

25

*Leave T2, the 10KΩ base resistor and the wire on S1 and H¹1 in place from page 21.
**The circuit diagram is on page 45.

Digital electronics

There are two main kinds of electronics, called digital and analogue. Digital circuits use pulses of electricity, whereas analogue circuits use a stream of electricity that can have a smoothly varying voltage.

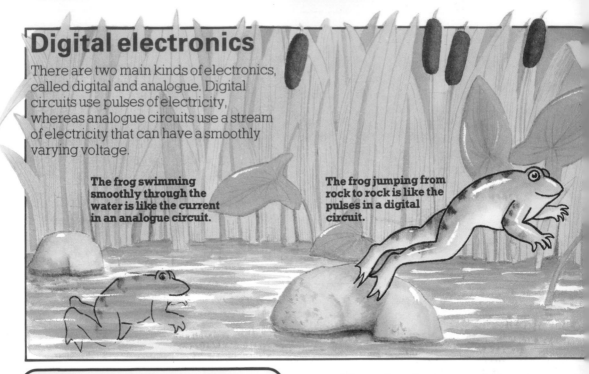

The frog swimming smoothly through the water is like the current in an analogue circuit.

The frog jumping from rock to rock is like the pulses in a digital circuit.

Digital and analogue signals

All the components in a circuit are receiving, sending or controlling small electric currents. These small currents are called signals and can be either digital or analogue, depending on how the circuit is designed. Patterns of signals can be used to switch parts of a piece of equipment on and off, or to represent information in code form.

An analogue signal is a current or voltage that varies smoothly.

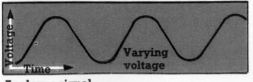

Analogue signal

A digital signal is a current or voltage which is either high or low, "on" or "off".

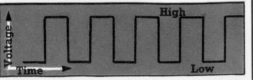

Digital signal

Switching circuits

Digital signals are created by switching circuits based on transistors. A complicated digital system, like that inside a computer, contains thousands of switching circuits.

Simple switching circuits are often called flip-flops. The type of flip-flop in the computer's memory is called a bistable switch. Bistable means that the circuit will stay either on or off, like a light switch.

Once it has been switched, you could say that the flip-flop "remembers" to stay on or off.

Digital electronics is usually thought of as a modern science, but Morse code, which was invented by 1836, uses pulses of current to transmit coded information along a wire.

The very latest technology, such as satellites, computers and robots, is controlled by digital circuits. Below, you can find out how digital circuits can control a piece of equipment.

1 The computer's memory consists of thousands of microscopic flip-flops etched on silicon chips. By switching on and off, the circuits create streams of digital pulses which are the code the computer uses to represent data and instructions.

2 The computer's code is called binary. Binary is a number system that uses two digits, 1 and 0. For every flip-flop that is on, the computer registers 1, and for off it registers 0.

On = 1   Off = 0

3 Each flip-flop can store a binary digit, called a "bit" for short. In a home computer, each piece of information is coded as a binary number and then stored in groups of eight bits called a byte.

Make a bistable flip-flop

Solder the components listed opposite onto pins at the places marked on the board.* Connect up the battery and touch **Q1** with the wander lead. The LED should come on and stay on even when you remove the wander lead. Now touch **R13** and the LED should go off.

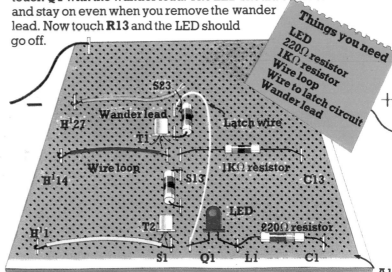

Things you need
LED
220Ω resistor
1KΩ resistor
Wire loop
Wire to latch circuit
Wander lead

The circuit is latched by the wire from the collector of T2 to the base of T1. This means that some of the output of the circuit is always being fed back to the input. The transistors control each other as explained on page 24. In this circuit there is a further sharing of the voltage through the latch. The wander lead always touches the collector of either transistor, which means you control by hand how the circuit switches. In a computer, this is done electronically.

27

*Unsolder any components no longer needed from the circuit on page 25.

More digital circuits

The bistable flip-flop on the previous page is a digital switching circuit that can stay on or off. On these two pages you can find out about two other kinds of digital circuits called monostable and astable.

A monostable circuit stays off until triggered by a current. When activated, it stays on for a period of time and then comes back to its starting position.

"Mono" comes from the Greek word *monos*, meaning single.

Doorbell

Pendulum

An astable switch will not stay in either position, but switches on and off all the time. A clock pendulum swinging to and fro behaves like an astable switch. Astable means "without a stable state".

Make a monostable timer

You can build a monostable timing circuit on the experiment board using a large capacitor and a resistor connected in series. By changing the collector load to a sounder, you could use it to time a boiled egg, or people's turns in a game.

Solder the components onto the pins marked in the picture below. Before connecting the battery, set the variable resistor about half-way. The wander lead is for re-setting the circuit, so hook this to one side for the moment.*

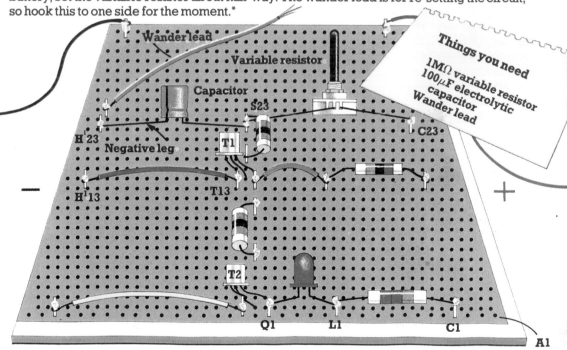

Wander lead
Variable resistor
Capacitor
S23
C23
H 23
Negative leg
T1
T13
H 13
T2
Q1
L1
C1
A1

Things you need
1MΩ variable resistor
100µF electrolytic capacitor
Wander lead

How to use the circuit

When you connect up the battery, the LED will light briefly, then go out. Ignore this, the circuit is just settling down. Now touch pin **S23** with the wander lead and the LED will come on. Take away the wander lead and the LED will stay on until the capacitor has charged up, then it goes out.

The capacitor and the variable resistor are dividing the voltage. Once the capacitor is charged, the circuit stays off until you re-set it by touching pin **S23** with the wander lead. Use the variable resistor to vary the time taken for the LED to go out.

*Remove the latch wire from the circuit on page 27.

Calculating the time

When circuit designers are working out an exact timing circuit, they use a formula to find the correct values of components to use.

TIME = CAPACITANCE × RESISTANCE
SECONDS = FARADS × OHMS

The calculations can be quite tricky for two reasons. Firstly, the transistor only needs 0.6 volts to switch on, and not the battery voltage, so working out the resistance with Ohm's law can be awkward.

Secondly, the time might be slightly out because the values of the components may be inaccurate. This is called component tolerance. You can buy very accurate components, but they are expensive and not necessary for this book.

The silver or gold stripe on a resistor tells you its tolerance.

Silver stripe

Gold stripe

Setting the time on your circuit

To make the circuit on the opposite page into a four minute timer, change the LED and resistor on pins **C1** and **Q1** for a piezo-electric sounder. Solder a 470Ω resistor onto pins **T13** and **H^{1}13**, in place of the wire. Set the variable resistor to the correct value by trial and error, using a watch.

Astable switching circuit

An astable circuit is made up of two monostables and switches on and off without staying in either position. Astable switches are used to control the pips on a speaking telephone clock, and to run the digital clock which regulates a computer's functions.

The way a see-saw goes up and down is like the current in an astable switching circuit.

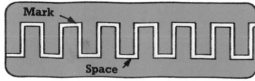

A relay works like a monostable switch because its contacts are only stable in their normal positions. Two relays wired together so that they switch one another on and off would make an astable switch.

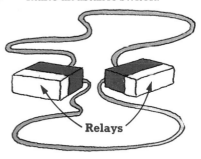

Relays

Frequency

The number of times an astable switch goes on and off in one second is called the frequency. Frequency is measured in units called hertz. Sometimes it is slow enough to count, but it can be thousands of times a second.

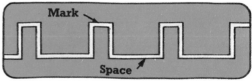

Mark

Space

Mark

Space

An astable circuit provides a fast changing voltage which can be drawn out in graphs like the ones above. They represent the "mark/space ratio" of the circuit. The lengths of the marks and the spaces change as you alter the values of the components. In the graph on the right, one of the transistors in the astable circuit is on longer than the other.

29

Amplifiers

An amplifier is a circuit which makes a small electric signal bigger. All electronic equipment that produces sound needs an amplifier to make it work. Transistors, which amplify current and voltage, are the most important components in an amplifier circuit.

Smooth analogue signal

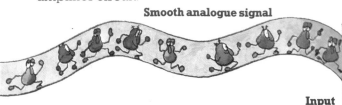

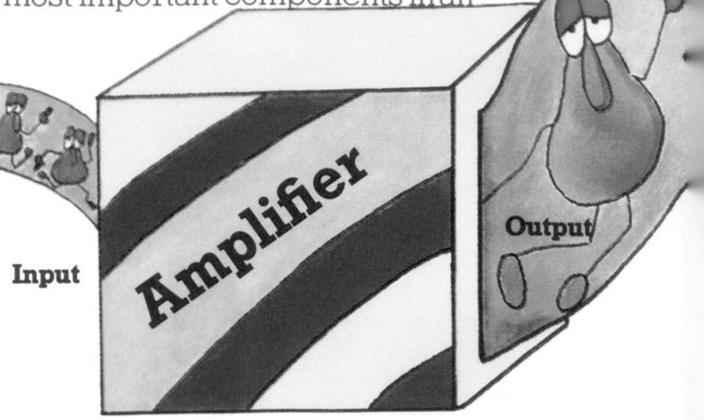

Input

Amplifier

Output

The signal received by the amplifier is called the input signal. It is usually a smooth, continuous analogue signal. An amplifier has faithfully to reproduce an enlarged version of the input signal. This is called the output of the amplifier circuit.

How the amplifier circuit works

This picture shows how the components in an amplifier circuit connect up and what they each do.

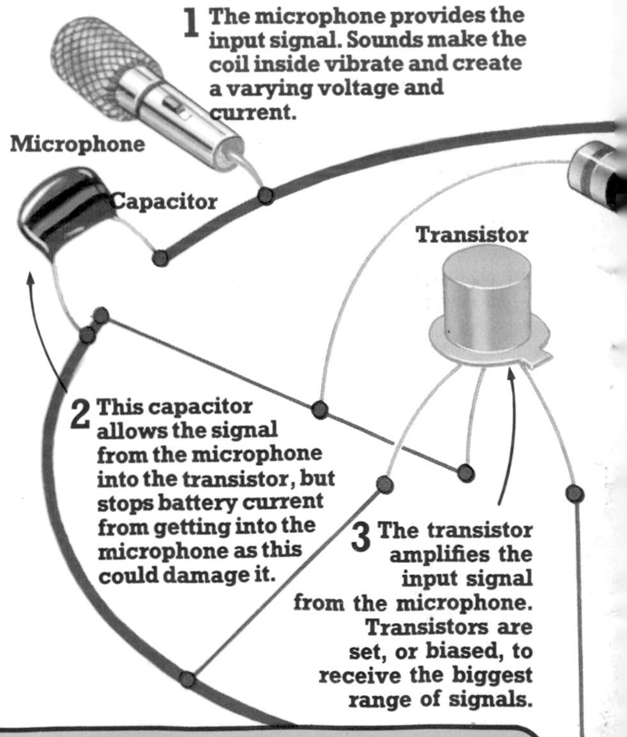

Follow the numbers to find out what each component does in the circuit.

Below, you can find out how the transistor is adjusted in an amplifier circuit.

1 The microphone provides the input signal. Sounds make the coil inside vibrate and create a varying voltage and current.

Microphone

Capacitor

Transistor

2 This capacitor allows the signal from the microphone into the transistor, but stops battery current from getting into the microphone as this could damage it.

3 The transistor amplifies the input signal from the microphone. Transistors are set, or biased, to receive the biggest range of signals.

Biasing the transistor

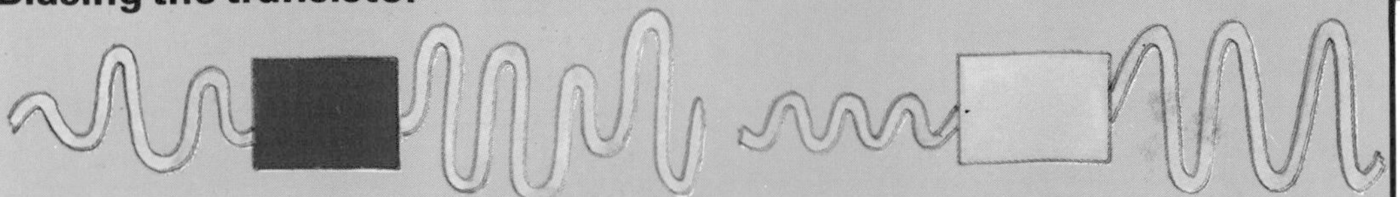

In an amplifier circuit, the transistor has to be set to half-on, so that it can receive the widest possible range of input signals.

Setting the transistor so that its condition is right is called biasing. All you need to bias the transistor is the correct value of resistor at the base.

Making sound into electricity

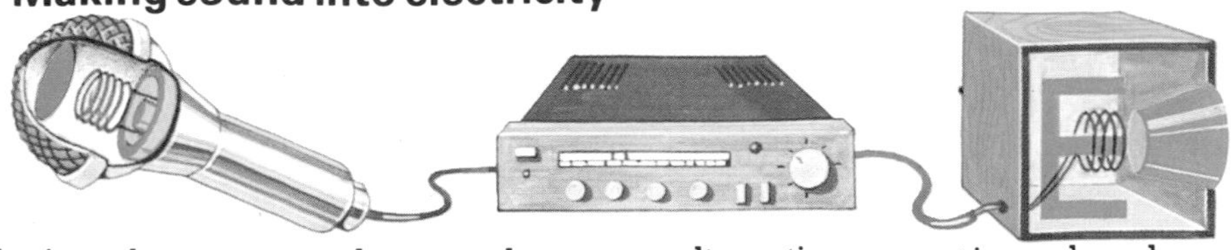

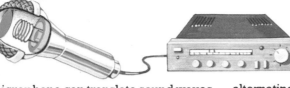

A microphone can translate sound waves into an alternating current (a.c.), which has a varying voltage. It contains a flat disk which vibrates when sound waves hit it. The vibrations are passed to a wire coil. Next to the coil there is a magnet. When the wire coil moves near a magnet, an alternating current is produced.

This input signal is made bigger by the amplifier, then passed to the loudspeaker. The loudspeaker also contains a wire coil and a magnet. The coil vibrates, making a paper cone vibrate and produce sound waves in the air.

This picture shows what each component does in an amplifier circuit. The components are not connected like this in an actual circuit.

Resistor

4 This resistor makes sure the transistor can handle input and output signals without causing distortion. It is called a feedback resistor. It is also serving as the base resistor.

5 This capacitor stops battery current from getting into the loudspeaker.

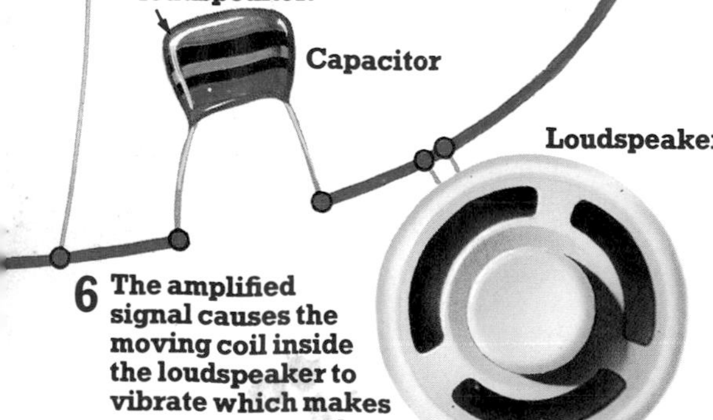

Capacitor

Loudspeaker

6 The amplified signal causes the moving coil inside the loudspeaker to vibrate which makes a paper cone produce sound waves in the air.

Because it can work like a microphone, a loudspeaker can also provide an input signal. You can use two loudspeakers for the input and output in the circuit on the right.

Clipping

When the input signal is too big, the top and bottom of the amplified signal gets chopped off by the transistor. This is called clipping. Imagine it like someone who keeps hitting their head on the ceiling and scraping their feet on the floor because their jump is too big. Clipping happens when a signal is fed back from the output to the input, making the input signal too big. This is called positive feedback and can cause distortion of the sound at the output.

More about the amplifier circuit

The circuit shown on these pages is called a single stage amplifier. It contains all the basic components of an amplifier circuit, but is not powerful enough to do any useful work on its own.

A more powerful amplifier, called a two-stage amplifier, consists mainly of two single stage amplifiers connected together. A two-stage amplifier has two transistors which amplify the input signal twice, which makes the output signal much stronger.

31

About the chip

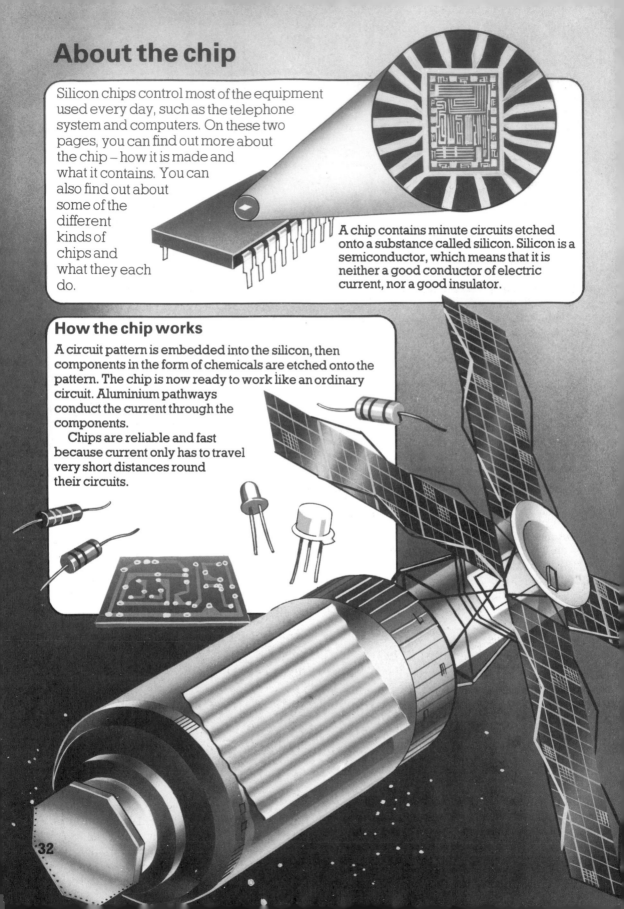

Silicon chips control most of the equipment used every day, such as the telephone system and computers. On these two pages, you can find out more about the chip – how it is made and what it contains. You can also find out about some of the different kinds of chips and what they each do.

A chip contains minute circuits etched onto a substance called silicon. Silicon is a semiconductor, which means that it is neither a good conductor of electric current, nor a good insulator.

How the chip works

A circuit pattern is embedded into the silicon, then components in the form of chemicals are etched onto the pattern. The chip is now ready to work like an ordinary circuit. Aluminium pathways conduct the current through the components.

Chips are reliable and fast because current only has to travel very short distances round their circuits.

Transistors on chips

Minute transistors are the main components on a chip and these do most of the work in controlling what the chip does. Some chips are digital and some analogue. The transistors etched onto digital chips function as switches and most of those on analogue chips are amplifiers.

On an analogue chip there are dozens of transistors and on a digital chip there are literally thousands.

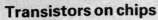

Different kinds of chip

There are many different kinds of chips used to do various jobs. One kind, called a microcomputer, contains enough circuits to control by itself equipment such as calculators, washing machines, or electronic games.

calculations and decisions which the computer makes.

The microprocessor needs memory chips so that it can store the information it receives. The interface chips convert the information typed into the computer into

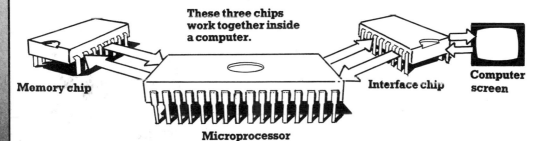

These three chips work together inside a computer.

Memory chip

Interface chip

Computer screen

Microprocessor

A more complicated piece of equipment, such as a home computer, contains more than one kind of chip. They work together to control the whole machine. The most important of those chips is the microprocessor, which carries out the

binary signals, and back again into information.

The computer also needs an electronic clock which keeps in order the thousands of calculations made by the computer every second.

A chipless world

If all the machines people use had been built using components the size of those used for experiments in this book, there probably would be no room for people in the world. The circuits in a digital watch

would fill a suitcase, home computers would be the size of swimming pools, and satellites would never get off the ground. Besides this, equipment would keep breaking down because chips are much more reliable than ordinary components.

The story of electronics

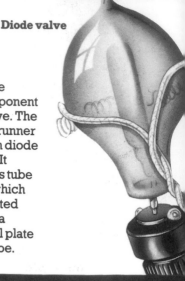

Electronics began only at the beginning of his century when the first electronic components were developed. It is a very young science compared with others such as physics and chemistry, which have been studied for hundreds of years. Already, however, the results of experiments in electronics have produced a technological revolution which has changed the world. On these two pages, you can find out about the first electronic components and the story of their development.

1 The first major development in electronics was the invention of a component called a diode valve. The valve was the forerunner of both the modern diode and the transistor. It consisted of a glass tube with wire inside, which when heated, emitted electrons through a vacuum* to a metal plate at the end of the tube.

5 Transistors are made of two kinds of semiconducting material called n-type and p-type. N and p refer to the special arrangement of the particles in the substance which may be either silicon or germanium.

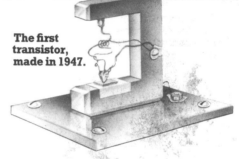

The first transistor, made in 1947.

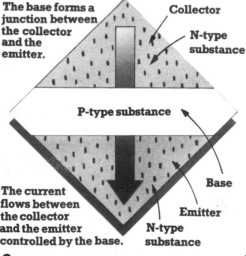

The base forms a junction between the collector and the emitter.

Collector

N-type substance

P-type substance

The current flows between the collector and the emitter controlled by the base.

Base

Emitter

N-type substance

4 Soon after, in the 1950s, the transistor was developed from the valve. It was small and solid, and needed no heat to make it work. Transistors gradually replaced valves in radios and TVs, and then in computers.

6 In 1958, the first chip was made by an American scientist called Jack Kilby. He put two transistors onto a silicon crystal. Since then, components and circuits have been miniaturized to fit as many as one million components onto one chip. This is possible through the development of methods of microscopic engraving on silicon. With further refinement of the technique of making them, more and more complex circuits can be made cheaply and reliably.

A tiny silicon chip

*A vacuum is a completely empty space.

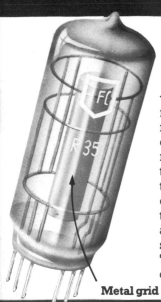

Triode valve

The electrons in the valve's tube could only flow in one direction, making the valve a diode. Later, a grid of metal was inserted into the valve which allowed the current to be controlled and varied so that the valve could also act as an amplifier or as a switch, like a transistor. This kind of valve was called a triode valve.

Metal grid

2 Valves were first used in radios, then in TVs, using their function as amplifiers.

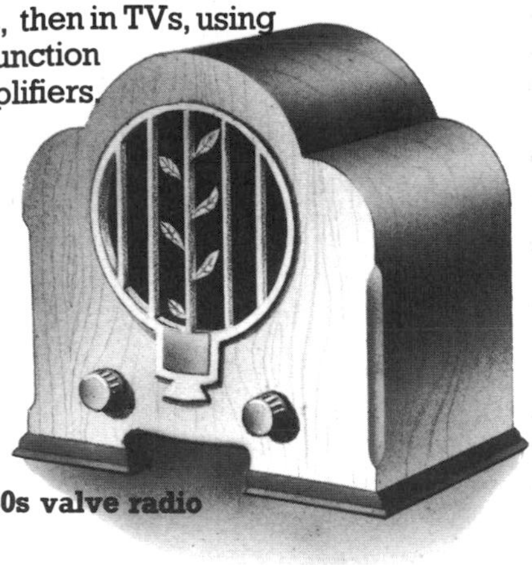

1930s valve radio

3 Later, in the 1940s, valves were used in the first computers, this time using their function as digital switches. The first computer contained 18,000 valves. It filled a whole room, and generated an enormous amount of heat, as each valve had to be heated in order to work.

This picture shows what the first room-sized computer looked like.

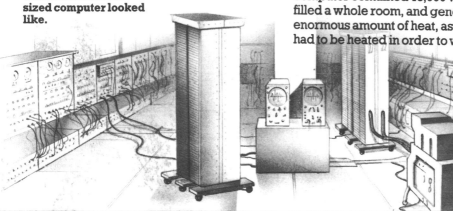

Before electronics

The first calculator, invented in 1821, had so many complicated mechanical cogs to operate it that it never actually worked. When valves were invented, all the cogs could be replaced by electronic circuits to do the calculations instead.

The first calculator, made by an English mathematician called Charles Babbage.

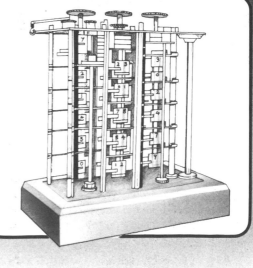

Testing and designing circuits

Testing circuits

You can buy test meters to help you work out the right value of components for a circuit, or to check for faults in a circuit.

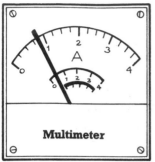
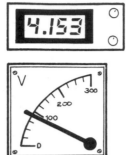

Multimeter

There are lots of different kinds of test meters, such as a voltmeter which measures voltage, an ammeter which measures current, or an ohmmeter which measures resistance. Meters which measure current, voltage and resistance, called multimeters, are also available.

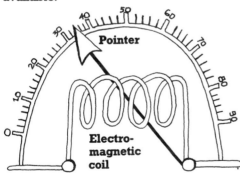

Pointer

Electro-magnetic coil

Inside most meters, there is a coil of wire near a strong magnet. The wire has a pointer attached to it. When a current goes through the coil, it creates another magnetic field and the coil turns. This moves the pointer to a number printed on a scale.

Designing circuits

A complicated electronic circuit is always made by joining up lots of simple circuits and making them work together.

Circuit symbols are used to design circuits to see if they actually work before making them.

When designing a circuit, you need to use the laws of electronics to work out such things as the value of the components you need for the circuit. Below, there is a list of some laws that will help you if you want to design your own circuits.

Electronics laws

Power law
Power (watts) = Voltage(volts) × current(amps)

Ohm's law
Voltage(volts) = Current(amps) × Resistance(ohms)

$$\text{Transistor gain} = \frac{\text{Collector current}}{\text{Base current}}$$

Time (seconds) = Capacitance(farads) × Resistance(ohms)

Resistors in series
Total resistance = the sum of the resistors connected in series

Colour code computer program

Here is a computer program to help you identify resistors when building circuits. It tells you the value of a resistor when you type in the colours of the stripes, or the stripe colours when you type in the value. The program will also give you a complete listing of the colour code.

The program works on the computers listed below. Some need minor conversions which are shown by the symbols beside the program listing.

Spectrum   APPLE
C64   BBC/Electron
VIC-20   TRS 80 colour

How to use the program

Type in the program, then press RETURN (or your computer's equivalent word). This will give you three choices, called the "menu".

Press **A** if you simply want a list of the colours and their corresponding numbers.

Press **B** and then type the resistor's value if you want to find out what colour its stripes should be.

Press **C** and then type in the stripe colours if you want to know the value of a resistor in ohms.

Conversions

▲ **Spectrum**

```
360 IF I$=C$(J)(TO LEN(I$)) THEN LET F=1
    :LET C(I)=J-1
490 DIM C$(10,6):DIM C(3)
```

● **C64 and VIC-20**

```
470 PRINT CHR$(147)
```

■ **Apple**

```
470 HOME
```

```
10 GOSUB 490
20 GOSUB 470
30 PRINT "COLOUR CODES HELPER"
40 PRINT:PRINT "A. COLOUR CODES LIST"
50 PRINT "B. VALUE TO COLOURS"
60 PRINT "C. COLOURS TO VALUE"
70 PRINT:PRINT "TYPE IN A,B OR C"
80 INPUT I$
90 IF I$="A" THEN GOSUB 130
100 IF I$="B" THEN GOSUB 180
110 IF I$="C" THEN GOSUB 320
120 GOTO 20
130 GOSUB 470
140 PRINT "COLOUR CODES ARE :":PRINT
150 FOR I=1 TO 10
160 PRINT TAB(2);C$(I);TAB(14);I-1
170 NEXT I:GOSUB 450:RETURN
180 GOSUB 470
190 PRINT "WHAT VALUE":INPUT V
200 PRINT "WHAT MULTIPLIER":PRINT "M=MEGOHMS"
210 PRINT "K=KILOHMS":PRINT "O=OHMS"
220 INPUT M$
230 IF M$="M" THEN LET V=V*1E6
240 IF M$="K" THEN LET V=V*1E3
250 LET NZ=0
260 IF V>=100 THEN LET V=V/10:LET NZ=NZ+1
    :GOTO 260
270 LET V=INT(V):PRINT:PRINT "COLOUR CODING IS"
280 PRINT C$(INT(V/10)+1);" ";
290 PRINT C$((V/10-INT(V/10))*10+1.1);" ";
300 PRINT C$(NZ+1):GOSUB 450
310 RETURN
320 GOSUB 470
330 FOR I=1 TO 3
340 PRINT "TYPE COLOUR ";I:INPUT I$
350 LET F=0:FOR J=1 TO 10
▲360 IF I$=C$(J) THEN LET F=1:LET C(I)=J-1
370 NEXT J:IF F=0 THEN PRINT "CHECK SPELLING"
    :GOTO 340
380 NEXT I
390 LET V=(C(2)+10*C(1))*10^C(3):LET M$=""
400 IF V>=1E6 THEN LET V=V/1E6:LET M$="MEG"
410 IF V>=1E3 AND M$<>"MEG" THEN LET V=V/1E3
    :LET M$="KIL"
420 PRINT:PRINT "VALUE IS ";V;" ";M$;"OHMS"
430 GOSUB 450
440 RETURN
450 PRINT:PRINT "PRESS RETURN TO CONTINUE"
460 INPUT X$:RETURN
●■470 CLS
480 PRINT:RETURN
▲490 DIM C$(10):DIM C(3)
500 FOR I=1 TO 10:READ C$(I):NEXT I
510 RETURN
520 DATA "BLACK","BROWN","RED"
530 DATA "ORANGE","YELLOW","GREEN"
540 DATA "BLUE","PURPLE","GREY"
550 DATA "WHITE"
```

Shopping list

On these two pages there is a complete shopping list for all the circuits in this book. You can buy the components all at once, or as you need them for each circuit. There is a checklist of components beside each circuit in this book. The list itemizes only the new components that are used, which means that you have to be very careful

that all the components needed from a previous circuit are still in place. The circuits are designed so that you can start at the beginning and work through, gradually building more complicated circuits from the basic ones. If you decide to build just one circuit, check carefully to make sure you do not miss anything out.

It is a good idea to buy extra components, especially resistors, transistors and LEDs. Resistors are used frequently in the book, and transistors and LEDs are easily damaged.

Full list of components

Resistors

¼watt, or ⅛watt, carbon composition.

$2 \times 100\Omega$

$2 \times 220\Omega$

$1 \times 470\Omega$

$4 \times 10K\Omega$

$2 \times 1K\Omega$

$1 \times 100K\Omega$

Special resistors

$1 \times$ rod thermistor

(High resistance, Negative Temperature Coefficient).

$1 \times 1M\Omega$ variable resistor

$1 \times$ light dependant resistor (LDR)

Transistors

$4 \times BC108$, NPN

LED

$1 \times$ LED, 0.2″ diameter (red or green)

Capacitor

$1 \times 100\mu$ Farad electrolytic

Diodes

$1 \times$ any diode in the series 1N4001-1N4006 (do not use Zener diodes)

Piezo-electric sounder

$1 \times$ Piezo-electric sounder

Relay

Double-pole changeover, 12Vd.c., 280Ω

(Take this diagram of the pin layout if you are not sure what to buy, and show it to the shopkeeper.)

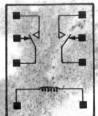

There are lots of mail order firms which sell electronic components and tools. Two useful addresses are listed below.

**Maplin Electronic Supplies Ltd.,
P.O. Box 3,
Rayleigh,
Essex, SS6 8LR,
U.K.**

**Tandy International Electronics,
1600 One Tandy Center,
Fort Worth,
Texas 76102,
U.S.A.**

In general, if you are in any doubt about how to identify any components, it is best to ask the shopkeeper when you buy the component. If necessary, take this book with you to the shop, and show the shopkeeper exactly what the components are for.

Tools and materials

1 × 0.1″ pitch Veroboard, 36 tracks × 50 holes.

1 × scrap piece of Veroboard of any size, on which to practise soldering.

Soldering iron (with a thin bit if possible).

A reel of multicore solder.

A 5mm drill bit.

5m (20′) "Bell" or "hook-up" wire.

Wire strippers

Wire cutters

Scissors

Paper
Glue
Cardboard
Aluminium foil

It is a good idea to look around your home for any useful tools and materials before buying them.

More about identifying components

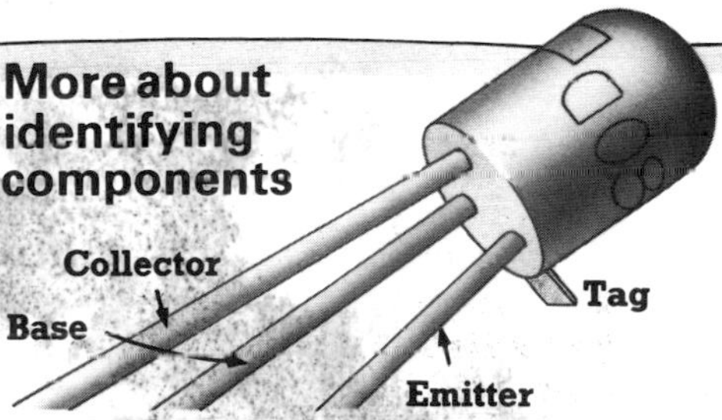

Collector

Base

Tag

Emitter

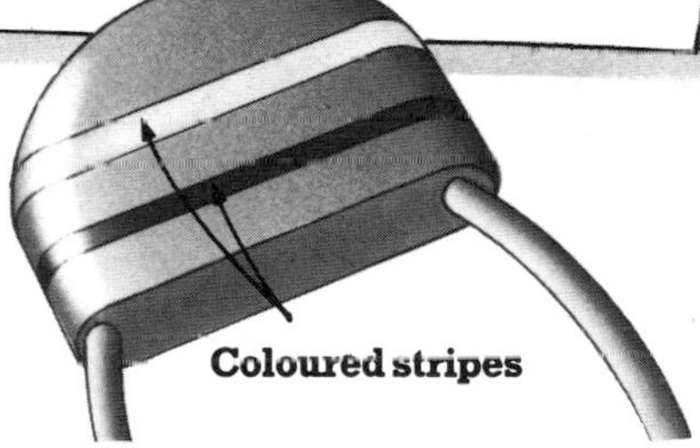

Coloured stripes

Transistors

The transistor (BC108), used in this book, is identified by the tag on the cap which is always nearest to the emitter.

Capacitors

Capacitors are identified either by colour-coded stripes or by numbers printed on them. Ask your supplier to help if you are not sure how to identify them.

Relay

The relay used for the burglar alarm circuit on page 25, has two contacts which are normally open and two which are normally closed. One of the normally closed contacts is used for latching the circuit, and one is used to switch on the bell.

When the relay switches on, the two normally open contacts close creating two paths for the current. The contact connected to the base of T1 latches the circuit, which stays on even when the burglar steps off the pressure mat.

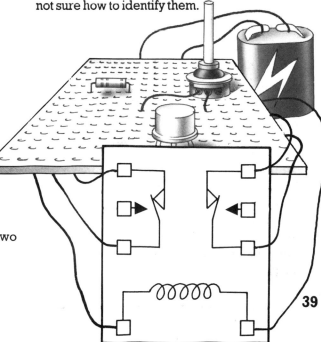

How to solder

Soldering is a way of joining two metals using a third metal called solder, which melts and makes a joint between them. On these two pages there is a step by step guide which tells you what you need for soldering, and how to go about it. It is a good idea to practise soldering before building any circuits. On pages 42-43, you can find out how to set up the experiment board that is used for the circuits in this book.

Things you need for soldering

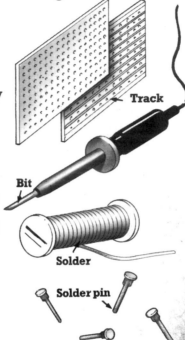

Track

Bit

Solder

Solder pin

Veroboard
Veroboard is a type of circuit board which has rows of holes, with copper tracks on the back. You fix components to the board by soldering them to the tracks, or to pins soldered to the tracks.

Multicore solder
This looks like long, thick wire. It is made of a mixture of metals that melt with the heat of the soldering iron. It hardens quickly to make a firm, shiny joint which secures the components to the board and can conduct current.

Soldering iron
A soldering iron has a pointed metal end called the bit. This becomes very hot and melts the solder. It is best to buy an iron with a bit no larger than the width of the track of the Veroboard. While the iron is hot, be very careful where you prop it up when you are not soldering.

Solder pins
These are tiny pins with heads at one end. They are made to fit the holes in the Veroboard exactly. You push them from the back to the front of the board, then solder the heads to the tracks.

It is a good idea to buy some resistors to practise soldering with as they are cheap and not easily damaged.

You also need a damp sponge to clean the bit of the iron before and after soldering.

Soldering on to pins

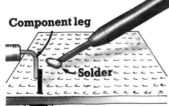

Component leg

Solder

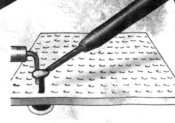

Take a solder pin and push it firmly from the back to the front of the board. Solder the pin head to the track to secure it.

Turn over the board so that it is front side up. Now wet the iron with some solder. Holding the iron in one hand, take the component in the other and hold its leg against the pin.

Now touch both the pin and the component's leg with the soldering iron. The blob of solder on the iron should be enough to join the leg to the pin.

How to solder

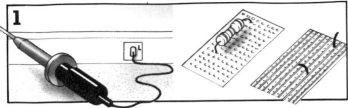

1

Plug in the soldering iron and wait for a few minutes. Make sure the bit is not touching anything, especially the mains lead.

Take a component and push its legs into holes on the front of a scrap piece of Veroboard. Bend the legs slightly.

2

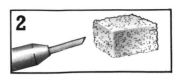

Clean the bit of the iron on a damp sponge.

3

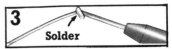

Solder

Now touch the bit with the solder to "wet" it.

4

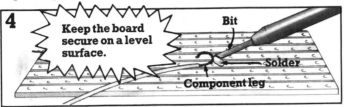

Keep the board secure on a level surface.

Bit

Solder

Component leg

Hold the bit against both the leg and the copper track. Keep the bit in place and touch the leg with the solder. The solder will melt and flow on to the track. Be careful! It only takes a second to melt.

5

Hold the board tilted away from you and carefully snip off the end of the leg with wirecutters.

6

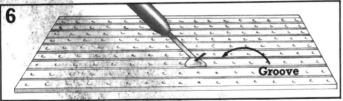

Groove

Check to make sure that no solder is joining two tracks. If so, clean the bit and run it firmly down the groove between the tracks until the groove is free from solder.

7 Check each joint carefully after soldering. It should look firm and shiny. A "dry" joint can stop a circuit from working. If it is not right, de-solder and try again.

De-soldering

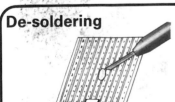

Hold the board firmly and point it away from you at a slight angle. Melt the soldered joint you want to remove and tap the board to flick off the solder.

Now push the leg from the back with the iron. With pliers, pull the component from the front and it should come free. Be careful as it is hot.

De-soldering from pins

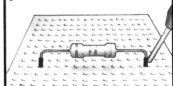

Hold the board and melt the joint between the component's leg and the pin. Pull the leg off the pin with pliers as the solder melts.

Preparing the experiment board

The experiment board is a piece of Veroboard on which you can build all of the circuits in this book. For each project you need to solder components to pins on the experiment board. To find the correct holes you can make a grid as described below. Unless otherwise stated, you keep the components from a previous project in place when you start a new one. On these two pages, you can find out how to set up the experiment board so that it is ready for all the circuits. It is a good idea to practise soldering first. There is a step-by-step guide on pages 40-41.

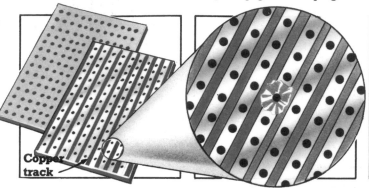

Copper track

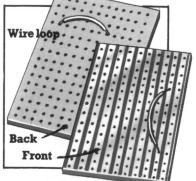

Wire loop

Back

Front

Veroboard is made from a non-conductive material. Current can only travel along the copper tracks in the back and through the components soldered to the tracks.

By breaking the copper track, you can divert current around a circuit to make it travel to components in the correct order. Find out on the opposite page how to break the track for the circuits in this book.

Sometimes you need to join tracks to allow current to flow between them. You do this by soldering a wire loop between the tracks to be joined. You can also use a wire loop to repair a split in the copper track.

Making a grid

The instructions for the circuits in this book use a letter and a number to represent every hole on the experiment board. This is to make it easier to find the right place for each component. The letters and numbers correspond to a grid which is stuck round two edges of the board at the front.

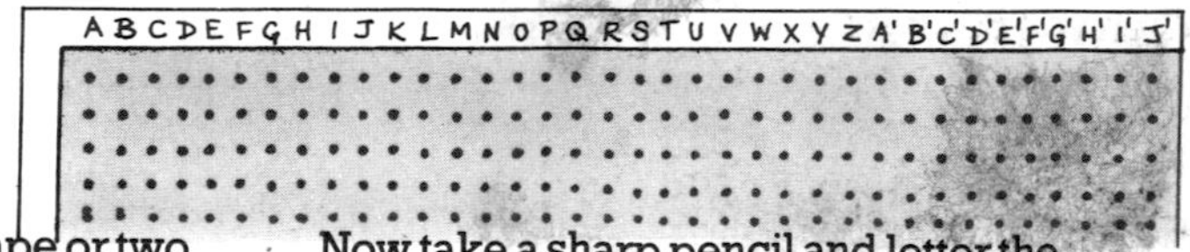

ABCDEFGHIJKLMNOPQRSTUVWXYZA'B'C'D'E'F'G'H'I'J'

To make a grid, use masking tape or two strips of paper. Stick a length of tape or paper round one long, and one short edge of the board.

Now take a sharp pencil and letter the shorter edge as shown above.

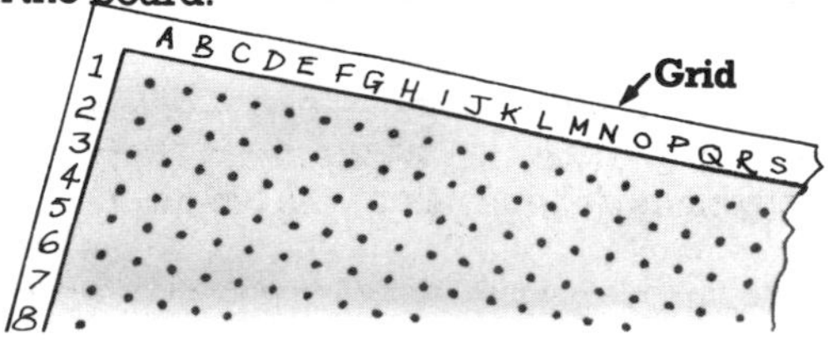

Grid

ABCDEFGHIJKLMNOPQRS

1 2 3 4 5 6 7 8

Tracks run this way.

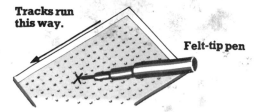

Felt-tip pen

Number the holes down the longer edge of the grid, 1 to 50. Careful! It is important to line up the numbers with the holes.

When you are building a circuit, it is a good idea to mark each hole as you find it with a felt-tip pen. This makes it easier to remember where it is.

Breaking the track

To break the track, you have to remove all the copper from the area round a hole at the back, or trackside, of the board.
You have to break the track for the circuits in this book. It is easier to do this before you begin, as the board is flat and free of components.

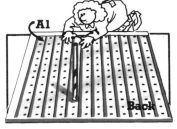

The breaks in the tracks listed cover all the circuits in the book.

Drill bit

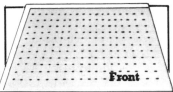

Front

Back

You can do this using a 4mm-6mm (⅛″-¼″) drill bit. Practise on a scrap piece of Veroboard, then break the track on the experiment board at the following holes: **L2, R7, R12, S12, L14, S19.**

Place the drill bit in the hole and turn it between your fingers until all the copper is removed from the track round the hole.

More than one component on pins

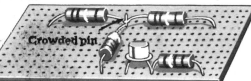

Crowded pin

Tracks run this way   Extra pin

In this book you will often find that there is more than one component leg to solder to each pin. This can be quite tricky. If there is room, you can push another solder pin into a hole on the same track as the crowded one, and solder the leg onto that instead. Make sure the extra pin is on the same track and not sending the current to the wrong part of the circuit. Check also that no other components or track breaks are between the two pins.

How to strip wire

When you buy wire, it is completely covered in plastic. Before you use it, you have to strip some plastic off both ends. To do this, it is best to use wire strippers. Adjust the strippers to fit the wire and pull off about 1cm (½″).

Stranded wire

Tinning

"Tinning" means coating a stripped piece of wire, or a component's leg with solder. Tinning helps to make good solder joints which give better conduction of current.

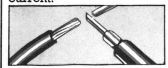

Tinned wire

Tinning wire

Keep the wire still by resting something heavy on it, then heat the stripped end with the iron. Now touch the hot wire with solder, running it gently along the length of exposed wire.

Warning

When you are soldering components on to pins, be very careful not to touch the components already on the board with the hot bit of the soldering iron. Transistors especially can be easily damaged by heat. It is a good idea to put the transistors in last when you are building a circuit.

43

Electronics words

Alternating current: Electric current that is constantly reversing its direction.

Ampere: The unit of current flow.

Analogue signal: A smoothly varying voltage or current.

Astable switch: A digital switching circuit that is not stable in either the on or the off position.

Bistable switch: A digital switching circuit that is stable in both the on or the off position.

Cathode Ray Oscilloscope (CRO): A meter, mostly used to measure and display electrical signals in graph form on a TV-like screen. A CRO can also measure the frequency of a.c., and a wide range of voltages.

Conductor: A substance through which an electric current can flow.

Coulomb: The unit that measures one ampere of current that flows for one second.

Current: A drift of electrons through a conductor such as a copper wire.

Digital signal: A signal which changes between high or low voltages with nothing in between.

Direct current: Current which flows constantly in one direction.

Electro-motive force (e.m.f.): A unit of electrical pressure very similar to voltage.

Electron: A negatively charged particle that orbits the nucleus of an atom.

Frequency: The measure of how often alternating current changes direction.

Impedance: Resistance which varies with the frequency of a signal. A loudspeaker, for instance, has no fixed resistance, but has an impedance measured in ohms.

Inductance: The property of a coil of wire to create a magnetic field that opposes the current that created it.

Input: The signal that is fed into a circuit or a component, e.g. a digital signal is the input to a bistable switching circuit.

Insulator: A substance through which electric current cannot flow.

Joules: The units which measure any kind of energy, e.g. electrical energy, mechanical energy.

NPN, PNP: How the different semiconductors, p-type and n-type, are arranged inside a transistor.

Oscillator: A circuit that moves backwards and forwards, such as an astable switch, and generates a signal of a certain frequency.

Output: The signal that comes out of a circuit or a component, e.g., the output signal from an amplifier circuit can be made into sound by going through a loudspeaker.

Potential difference (p.d.): An electric current can only flow between two points where there is a difference of electrical pressure between them. A battery, for instance, allows the current to flow because there is a potential difference between the terminals.

PNP: See NPN.

Saturation: Another way of saying the transistor is fully on. The point at which the transistor stops amplifying and there is no more gain.

Semiconductor: A substance which is neither a good conductor nor a good insulator, and will only conduct under certain conditions. E.g. silicon.

Signal: A voltage or current that is being used by a component or a circuit.

Transducer: A device that has the ability to change one form of energy to another, or vice versa, e.g. mechanical energy to electrical energy.

Transistor gain: The measurement of how much a base current is amplified by a transistor. It can be found by dividing the base current by the collector current.

Voltage: The measurement of potential difference between two points in a circuit, taking resistance into account.

Voltage division: The voltage applied to a chain of components connected in series is divided up in proportion to their resistances. (The sum of the voltages across each component equals the voltage applied to the chain.)

Watts: The units which measure the power of a circuit. Power can be found by multiplying the voltage by the current.

Circuit diagrams

Page 21 LDR circuit

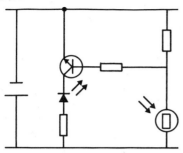

Page 23 Burglar alarm

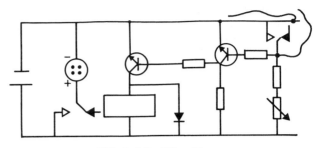

Page 26 Monostable flip-flop

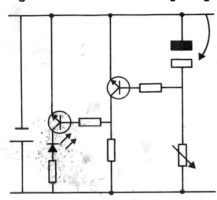

Page 25 Bistable flip-flop

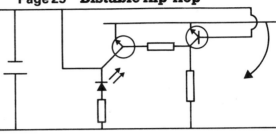

Answers to puzzles

Page 10:

a) 2000 ohms, or 2 Kilohms (red, black, red)

b) 12 ohms (brown, red, black)

Page 11:

4 amps of current

Page 24:

a) The sounder would ring in the dark because the LDR has a high resistance in the dark, making T1 off, and T2 on.

b) No, because T1 would be on and T2 off.

Make a pressure mat

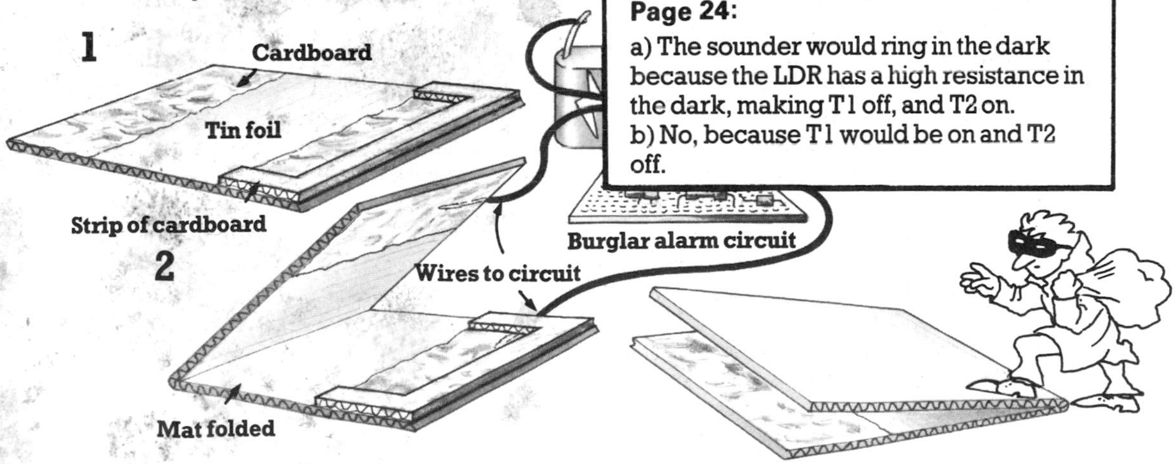

1

Cardboard

Tin foil

Strip of cardboard

2

Wires to circuit

Mat folded

Burglar alarm circuit

Here is an idea for a pressure mat to make for the circuit on page 25.

Take a stiff piece of cardboard and stick some tin foil to both ends on the same side. Fold the mat in half and tape a thin strip of cardboard on to one end to prevent the tin foil touching by accident.

Tape the pressure mat wires from the circuit on to the tin foil at either end of the pressure mat.

If a burglar steps on it, the two ends of the mat will touch and the tin foil will conduct the current between the pressure mat wires, switching on the circuit.

Faults checklist

Circuits are very fragile and fiddly to build and a tiny mistake can prevent a circuit from working. Although the fault is usually small, it can be difficult to find it. Use the checklist below to identify faults if your circuit does not work. Carefully re-check everything if it still does not work.

On the things you need list for each circuit, the components already on the board from a previous circuit are not listed again. Before beginning a new circuit, check carefully that the components are still in place from the last one.

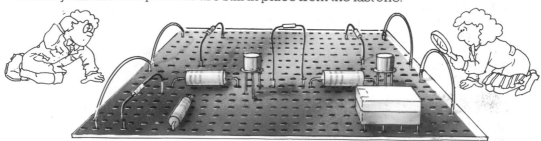

1 Are all the components in the right places on the board or on their pins?

2 Have you left off any of the components? It is easy to forget something in the circuits which have lots of components.

2 TRANSISTORS
4 LED
6 RESISTORS
WIRE
DIODES

3 Are all the solder joints firm? Gently pull each component to make sure nothing is loose.

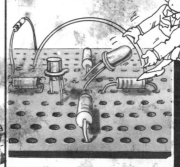

4 A dull solder joint is called a "dry" joint, and could stop a circuit from working. Check that all the solder joints are shiny.

5 Check that you have broken the track behind all the holes listed on page 43.

6 Make sure all transistors, electrolytic capacitors, diodes and LEDs are connected the right way round. If a transistor, for instance, is connected with its legs in the wrong hole, it may be damaged. If so, try re-soldering it the correct way round first, and if the circuit still does not work use another transistor.

7

Components may have been damaged by heat from the soldering iron. Transistors are often damaged by heat and you have to be extra careful when soldering components on to pins near a transistor. Replace any transistor which may have been affected by this.

8

Check to make sure all components are of the correct value. If the resistors, for instance, are too high, they may not be allowing enough current to flow.

9

Check that no tracks are joined by solder. If so, run the bit of the soldering iron firmly between the tracks until the groove is clear.

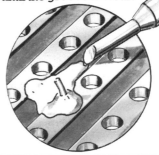

10

Check to see if any legs or bits of wire are touching each other on the board. This could be causing a short circuit. (See right.)

11

Check each track on the experiment board for cracks. Re-connect the track with wire over any crack to complete the current path.

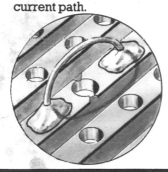

Short circuits

A short circuit happens when there is a connection from one part of a circuit to another which allows the current to flow through components the wrong way, or through the wrong components.
This can happen if you forget to break the track or if components' legs are touching each other on the board.

Warning

Do not use thick wire, e.g. mains wire, to build your projects. It is difficult to attach thick wire securely to the pins on the board, especially if you are making a short connection. It could also touch other components and cause a short circuit. (See pages 38-39 for the best kind of wire to buy.)

 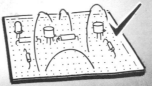

Go through this checklist twice. Ask someone else to check the position of each component. If you still cannot find the fault, wrap your circuit up carefully and send it with a stamped addressed envelope, and a description of the problem, to:

Electronics Adviser,
Usborne Publishing Ltd,
20, Garrick Street,
London WC2E 9BJ

Index

Printed in Belgium